Performance Tasks, Checklists, and Rubrics

Cindy Stergar

CORWIN PRESS
A SAGE Publications Company
Thousand Oaks, CA 91320

For information:

Corwin Press
A Sage Publications Company
2455 Teller Road
Thousand Oaks, California 91320
www.corwinpress.com

Sage Publications Ltd.
1 Oliver's Yard
55 City Road
London EC1Y 1SP
United Kingdom

Sage Publications India Pvt. Ltd.
B-42, Panchsheel Enclave
Post Box 4109
New Delhi 110 017 India

Printed in the United States of America.

Library of Congress Cataloging-in-Publication Data

ISBN 1-5751-7857-5

This book is printed on acid-free paper.

07   08   09   10   11   10   9   8   7   6   5   4   3   2   1

DEDICATION

I dedicate this book to all of the Teacher Leadership Academy teachers who have taken on the challenge of continuous improvement and tried to do things differently because it was the right thing to do for students. Their commitment, creativity, and persistence have been a powerful inspiration that changed my life.

Someone once said that a single snowflake didn't make a bit of difference, but when they all got together they could stop an interstate. The Teacher Leadership Academy teachers have done it! Every single teacher made a difference, and together they are unbelievable. Let it snow, let it snow, let it snow!

Contents

Foreword

The legacy that Cindy Litts Stergar left upon her passing was how she helped literally thousands of teachers transform their classrooms into centers of learning. Chief among her many shared research theories and practices was the use of rubrics as a means of measuring the degree by which learning was taking place. Through synthesizing the works of Kay Burke and a number of other educational authorities on rubrics, Cindy developed her own format style and created a compilation of rubric samples from teachers that other teachers could adopt or adapt for their own classrooms. The legacy of changing the classroom experiences of thousands of teachers was accomplished in large part through the Teacher Leadership Academy that Cindy developed and led over a period of eight years preceding her death. The Teacher Leadership Academy's goal was and still is to keep teachers at the top of their game regarding the research, trends, and skills necessary for today's classrooms. It was through the Teacher Leadership Academy that Cindy obtained numerous rubric samples from teachers participating in the Academy. Cindy created this compilation of teacher-prepared rubrics during the last months of her battle with breast cancer that took her life on September 21, 2001. Cindy believed that the "responsibility for knowing is sharing." She leaves this book as her legacy of sharing the knowledge and works of other teacher leaders.

TOM PAGAN
EXECUTIVE DIRECTOR,
CENTRAL INDIANA EDUCATIONAL SERVICE CENTER

Acknowledgments

A million thanks to my wonderful family: my optimistic and loving husband, Mark Stergar, who holds my hand every day and encourages me; my young daughter, Vicky, who has always been an inspiration to change things; and my older children, Jesi, Emily, and Jacob, who are successful in college now and can see clearly what was missing in K–12 and tell me so I can try to "fix it." Thank you also to my parents, Stan and Angie Litts, for their love and encouragement and for making me an avid reader and nurturing a gentle heart within me.

I have had the honor of working in professional development with many teachers who have profoundly influenced my thinking. The Teacher Leadership Academy through the Central Indiana Educational Service Center has been the greatest, most sustained learning environment for developing ideas that I have ever been a part of. I wish to thank the nearly 500 master teachers who have participated in the program so far for their courage and bright ideas; the executive director, Tom Pagan, for his vision and the words "just go do it," which enabled me to author and direct the program; and my invaluable assistant and dear friend, Mary Brabson, for making everything happen "just right."

This book would not be a reality without the grace of God and two very special doctors, Dr. George Sledge and Dr. Provine Mathur of University Hospital in Indianapolis. Their brilliance enabled me to be here. I am forever indebted to them and thank them for being the kind of brilliant minds we as educators need desperately to enrich.

Kay Burke for her wonderful insight and encouragement and for paving the way as the pioneer of creative rubrics; to Carol Luitjens for her wisdom, vision, and confidence in my ideas; and to Sue Schumer for never giving up on me, always being patient and kind, and believing in this book.

Introduction

This book is a practical guide for teachers interested in aligning their assessments with curricular and instructional goals, including national, state, and local standards. Teachers are introduced to three methods of authentic assessment—performance tasks, checklists, and rubrics. These methods allow students to demonstrate mastery of content beyond traditional tests and letter grades.

While traditional grading remains a part of the educational system, criteria and standards that represent students' knowledge are far more important and must be clearly defined in the instructional and assessment process. Standards-based learning requires teachers to find assessments that measure students' ability to meet the standards. Performance tasks, checklists, and rubrics are specifically designed to measure standards-based learning.

Performance tasks, checklists, and rubrics provide a customized, detailed, creative, and student-centered approach to assessment. When authentic assessments are used, students know what is expected of them as they begin a unit, and they understand how their performance, project, or product measured up as they complete a unit. Instead of receiving a letter grade with no explanation, students receive a detailed analysis of their performance, project, or product. This book explains how teachers can use these assessment tools to authentically assess student learning and to align learning with curriculum and instructional goals.

This book features five chapters focusing on various aspects of assessment tools. Chapter 1 provides an integrated look at the cornerstones of teaching—curriculum, instruction, and assessment. Teachers examine the programs, methods, and choices available to them during curriculum and instructional planning and how their choices relate to one another. Teachers are also introduced to the assessment measures that are explained further in the rest of the book.

Chapter 2 examines the performance task and explains how this tool can be used as part of the assessment process. Teachers learn what performance tasks are and how to create them. Examples of performance tasks for elementary, middle, and high school are featured.

Chapter 3 introduces the checklist, a measurable list of categories and indicators for projects, products, and performances. Teachers learn how to align the checklist with learning standards and goals and how to follow a step-by-step process to create an effective checklist. Sample checklists for elementary, middle, and high school are provided.

Chapter 4 introduces a key assessment tool, the rubric. Teachers learn how to create rubrics that effectively measure students' knowledge in alignment with standards. Sample rubrics for elementary, middle, and high school are featured.

Chapter 5 summarizes how these different assessment tools can be applied in the classroom on a daily basis, together or separately.

The appendices feature sample assessment tools that you may adopt or modify for use in your own classroom. Appendix A includes several assessment sets; each set features a performance task, one or two checklists, and a rubric. Appendix B includes sample rubrics in a variety of formats. These assessment sets and rubrics were written by practicing K–12 teachers. They represent a wide variety of styles, content, and grade levels.

Creating assessment tools is hard work. In an effort to work smarter, rather than harder, many teachers engage in share fairs, trading parties, and listservs in which they share assessment tools and ideas with colleagues. (Imagine creating a rubric, sharing it with 60 colleagues, and receiving 60 rubrics in return!) The hope is that this book will inspire teachers to create their own assessments, share their assessments with other teachers, inspire those teachers to create and share assessments, and so on.

CHAPTER 1

Curriculum, Instruction, and Assessment

In today's classroom, it seems obvious how important the cornerstones of teaching—curriculum and instruction—are to learning. But where does assessment fit into the picture? Is it just an add-on to the cornerstones?

Assessment is every bit as important as curriculum and instruction because it serves as a critical communication tool between teacher and student. When teachers use assessments correctly, they provide students with feedback and invite students to take the next step in their learning journeys. Because assessment is so crucial to good instruction, it is a critical responsibility of the teacher.

Madeline Hunter (1981) referred to teaching as a constant stream of decision making. Assessment is a part of this decision-making process that combines curriculum and instruction. In this chapter, we examine curriculum, instruction, and assessment in order to fully understand the choices and challenges teachers face in preparing to teach.

CURRICULUM

Teachers throughout the nation have been tasked with merging national standards, state standards, curriculum guides, and age-appropriate teaching materials. One of their biggest challenges is to provide substantive learning and avoid merely "covering" the prescribed material. Although teachers know that they must teach students the content that will appear on high-stakes tests, they also realize that students must be able to transfer their knowledge to other subjects and to life outside of school. Teachers must avoid overcrowding the curriculum while still ensuring that students can meet the standards.

Curriculum Mapping

One way to align standards and curriculum is curriculum mapping. Heidi Hayes Jacobs (1997) pioneered the concept of curriculum mapping as a way to communicate and visually display standards, content, skills, projects, objectives, and assessment strategies (e.g., case studies, performance-based learning, project-based learning, service learning, and thematic units). Teachers can use a curriculum map to select appropriate content and sequence the content so that it fits with the rest of the K–12 learning experience. Figure 1.1 shows a sample curriculum map for grade 7 curricular choices. Use Figure 1.2 to create your own curriculum map.

FIGURE 1.1   Sample Curriculum Map

	LANGUAGE ARTS	SOCIAL STUDIES	SCIENCE	MATHEMATICS
September	Diary of Anne Frank	The Westward Movement	Interactions and Changes	Problem Solving
October				Decimals
November	Sarah Plain and Tall	The Civil War	Diversity of Living Things	Data Analysis
December				Fractions
January	To Kill a Mockingbird	Industrial Revolution, World War I	Force and Motion	Integers
February	Johnny Tremain		The Restless Earth	Rations/Percents
March	Paul Bunyan and the Winter of the Blue Snow	The Great Depression	The Universe	Probability
April		World War II		Geometry
May	The Raven and the Coming of Daylight		Solutions	Intro to Algebra

Adapted from Jacobs, H. (1997). *Mapping the big picture.* Alexandria, VA: Association for Supervision and Curriculum Development.

FIGURE 1.2	Curriculum Map Template			
	LANGUAGE ARTS	SOCIAL STUDIES	SCIENCE	MATHEMATICS
September				
October				
November				
December				
January				
February				
March				
April				
May				

From Williams, B. R., & Dunn, S. (2000). *Brain-compatible learning for the block.* Thousand Oaks, CA: Corwin Press. Used with permission.

Curriculum Integration

Another way to align content and standards is curriculum integration. Teachers may integrate the curriculum by creating a unit that teaches a number of standards and that helps students transfer knowledge beyond the unit and into life. Curricular integration ensures that essential content is presented and that students make connections and understand the context of various processes (Jacobs, 1997). When ideas are connected across curricular areas, students can see the relationships among and between disciplines, which helps to build their understanding (Fogarty, 1991). Integration also allows teachers to cover several standards in a short amount of time.

There are several different models teachers can use to integrate the curriculum. Figure 1.3 demonstrates ten models for integrating the curriculum, varying from integration within a single discipline (cellular model) to integration across several disciplines (threaded model) to integration within the learner (networked model) (Fogarty, 1991).

Alignment by the Book

Textbooks, no matter how wonderful, should be viewed merely as helpful resources in the standards-based curriculum. Instead of merely covering the content, teachers are now encouraged to organize instruction around core concepts (National Research Council, 2000).

The challenges are clear. Very few schools have chosen to build curriculum writing and professional development into the schedule. And those who have tend to allow only a few hours here and there or a few half-day sessions to be devoted to curriculum development. These haphazard approaches do not enable teachers to engage in the consistent, rigorous work needed to produce a sound curriculum that has clearly defined instructional units and aligned assessments.

However, teachers can find many excellent resources that will help them align curriculum and standards. Many national organizations have published content-specific standards in detailed formats (see Figure 1.4). Most states have adopted standards that reflect the content of their state tests. (See Figure 1.5 for a list of Internet links to specific state content standards.)

By using techniques such as curriculum mapping, curricular integration, and aligning standards, teachers can teach the curriculum in a way that results in meaningful instruction for their students.

FIGURE 1.3 Ten Models for Integrating the Curriculum

1 Cellular
Periscope—one direction; one sighting; narrow focus on single discipline or content area

Description
The traditional model of separate and distinct disciplines, as depicted by student learning standards in each discipline area.

Example
The teacher applies this view in mathematics, science, social studies, language arts or sciences, humanities, fine and practical arts.

2 Connected
Opera glass—details of one discipline; focus on subtleties and interconnections

Description
Within each subject area, course content is connected topic to topic, concept to concept, one year's work to the next, and relates ideas explicitly.

Example
The teacher relates the concept of fractions to decimals, which in turn relates to money, grades, etc.

3 Nested
3-D glasses—multiple dimensions to one scene, topic or unit

Description
Within each subject area, the teacher targets multiple skills: a social skill, a thinking skill, and a content-specific skill based on standards.

Example
The teacher designs the unit on photosynthesis to simultaneously target consensus seeking (social skill), sequencing (thinking skill), and plant life cycle (science content).

4 Sequenced
Eye glasses—varied internal content framed by broad, related topics

Description
Topics or units of study are rearranged and sequenced to coincide with one another. Similar ideas are taught in concert while remaining separate subjects.

Example
An English teacher presents a historical novel depicting a particular period while the history teacher teaches that same historical period.

5 Shared
Binoculars—two disciplines that share overlapping concepts and skills

Description
Shared planning takes place in two disciplines in which overlapping concepts or ideas emerge as organizing elements.

Example
Science and mathematics teachers use data collection, charting, and graphing as shared concepts.

6 Webbed
Telescope—broad view of an entire constellation as one theme, webbed to the various elements

Description
Webbed curricula represent the thematic approach to integrating subject matter.

Example
The teacher presents a simple topical theme, such as the circus, and webs it to the subject areas. A conceptual theme, such as conflict, can be webbed for a broader thematic approach.

7 Threaded
Magnifying glass—big ideas that magnify all content through a metacurricular approach

Description
Standards, thinking skills, social skills, study skills, graphic organizers, technology, and a multiple intelligences approach to learning thread through all disciplines.

Example
The teaching staff targets prediction in reading, mathematics, and science lab experiments while the social studies teacher targets predicting current events, and thus threads prediction across all four disciplines.

8 Integrated
Kaleidoscope—new patterns and designs that use the basic elements of each discipline

Description
The integrated curricular model represents a cross-disciplinary approach similar to the shared model.

Example
In mathematics, science, social studies, fine arts, language arts, and practical arts, teachers look for patterns and approach content through these patterns in all the discipline areas.

9 Immersed
Microscope—intensely personal view that allows microscopic exploration as all content is filtered through lens of interest and expertise

Description
The individual integrates all data, from every field and discipline, by funneling the ideas through his or her area of interest.

Example
A student or doctoral candidate has an area of expert interest and sees all learning through that lens.

10 Networked
Prism—a view that creates multiple dimensions and directions of focus

Description
The networked model of integrated learning is an ongoing external source of input, forever providing new, extended, and extrapolated or refined ideas.

Example
An architect, while adapting the CAD/CAM technology for design, networks with technical programmers and expands her knowledge base, just as she had traditionally done with interior designers.

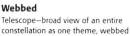

From Fogarty, R. (1991). *The mindful school: How to integrate the curricula.* Palatine, IL: IRI/Skylight Publishing, Inc. [Note: Fogarty extrapolated this model from Jacobs, H. H. (Ed.). (1989).] *Interdisciplinary curriculum: Design and implementation.* Alexandria, VA: Association for Supervision and Curriculum Development.)

| FIGURE 1.4 | **Resources for Content Standards** |

Technology

International Society for Technology in Education. (2000). *National educational technology standards for students.* Retrieved February 27, 2004, from http://cnets.iste.org/students/s_stands.html

International Society for Technology in Education. (2000). *National educational technology standards for teachers.* Retrieved February 27, 2004, from http://cnets.iste.org/teachers/t_stands.html

Science

National Academy of Sciences. (1996). *National science education standards.* Washington, DC: National Academy Press. (An electronic version of the standards is available at http://www.nap.edu/books/ 0309053269/html/index.html)

Language Arts

National Council of Teachers of English. (1996). *Standards for the English language arts.* Newark, DE: International Reading Association; Urbana, IL: National Council of Teachers of English.

Mathematics

National Council of Teachers of Mathematics. (2000). *Principles and standards for school mathematics.* Reston, VA: Author. (A 90-day, free trial electronic version of the standards is available at http:// standards.nctm.org)

Social Studies

National Council for the Social Studies. (1994). *Expectations of excellence: Curriculum standards for social studies and standards for the preparation of social studies teachers.* Silver Spring, MD: Author.

Visual Arts

National Art Education Association. (1994). *The national visual arts standards.* Reston, VA: Author.

General Curriculum Resources*

Center for Education Reform
http://edreform.com/standard.htm
This site offers links to standards and curriculum resources in many content areas. Click on "Standards and Curriculum Resources" at the bottom of the home page. Use links to search for content and state standards.

Interstate New Teacher Assessment and Support Consortium Standards Development
http://www.ccsso.org/projects/interstate_new_teacher_assessment_and_support_consortium/Projects/ Standards_Development/
This site offers core standards for new teachers and standards for arts education, elementary education, English language arts, foreign languages, mathematics, science, social studies, and special education.

---

*General curriculum resources adapted from Ronis, D. (2002). *Clustering standards in integrated units.* Thousand Oaks, CA: Corwin Press.

FIGURE 1.5   State Content Standards

Alabama http://www.alsde.edu/html/sections/ section_detail.asp?section=54

Alaska http://www.educ.state.ak.us/ ContentStandards/home.html

Arizona http://www.ade.state.az.us/standards/

Arkansas http://arkedu.state.ar.us/ standards/index.html

California http://www.cde.ca.gov/challenge/

Colorado http://www.cde.state.co.us/index_stnd.htm

Connecticut http://www.state.ct.us/sde/

Delaware http://www.doe.state.de.us/DPIServices/ DOE_Standards.htm

District of Columbia http://www.k12.dc.us/dcps/ curriculum/curriculum1.html

Florida http://www.firn.edu/doe/menu/sss.htm

Georgia http://www.doe.k12.ga.us/index.asp

Hawaii http://www.hcps.k12.hi.us/

Idaho http://www.sde.state.id.us/Dept/

Illinois http://www.isbe.net/ils/

Indiana http://ideanet.doe.state.in.us/standards/ welcome.html

Iowa http://www.state.ia.us/educate/ecese/nclb/ doc/ccsb.html

Kansas http://www.ksbe.state.ks.us/assessment/

Kentucky http://www.education.ky.gov/KDE/ Instructional+Resources/Curriculum+Documents +and+Resources/Core+Content+for+Assessment +-+version+3.0.htm

Louisiana http://www.doe.state.la.us/lde/ssa/ 1819.html

Maine http://www.state.me.us/education/ homepage.htm

Maryland http://mdk12.org/mspp/index.html

Massachusetts http://www.doe.mass.edu/ frameworks/

Michigan http://www.michigan.gov/mde/ 0,1607,7-140-6530_6568—,00.html

Minnesota http://education.state.mn.us/html/ intro_committee.htm

Mississippi http://www.mde.k12.ms.us/accred/ MPSAS.doc

Missouri http://www.dese.state.mo.us/standards/

Montana http://www.opi.state.mt.us/standards/

Nebraska http://www.nde.state.ne.us/ AcadStand.html

Nevada http://www.nde.state.nv.us/sca/ standards/index.html

New Hampshire http://www.ed.state.nh.us/ CurriculumFrameworks/curricul.htm

New Jersey http://www.state.nj.us/njded/stass/ index.html

New Mexico http://www.ped.state.nm.us/standards/ index.html

New York http://www.nysatl.nysed.gov/ standards.html

North Carolina http://www.dpi.state.nc.us/ student_promotion/

North Dakota http://www.dpi.state.nd.us/standard/ index.shtm

Ohio http://ims.ode.state.oh.us/ode/ims/ Default.asp?bhcp=1

Oklahoma http://www.sde.state.ok.us/publ/pass.html

Oregon http://www.ode.state.or.us/cifs/newspaper/

Pennsylvania http://www.pde.state.pa.us/ stateboard_ed/cwp/view.asp?a=3&Q=76716& stateboard_edNav=|5467|&pde_internetNav=|

Rhode Island http://www.ridoe.net/standards/

South Carolina http://www.sde.state.sc.us/ offices/cso/

South Dakota http://www.state.sd.us/deca/octa/ index.htm

Tennessee http://www.state.tn.us/education/ci/ cistandards.htm

Texas http://www.tea.state.tx.us/teks/

Utah http://www.uen.org/core/

Vermont http://www.state.vt.us/educ/new/html/ pubs/framework.html

Virginia http://www.pen.k12.va.us/go/Sols/ home.shtml

Washington http://www.k12.wa.us/ CurriculumInstruct/default.aspx

West Virginia http://wvde.state.wv.us/csos/

Wisconsin http://www.dpi.state.wi.us/dpi/ standards/index.html

Wyoming http://www.k12.wy.us/eqa/nca/ pubs/standards.asp

*General curriculum resources adapted from Ronis, D. (2002). *Clustering standards in integrated units.* Thousand Oaks, CA: Corwin Press.

INSTRUCTION

Instruction answers the question: How do I teach so that students learn? There are so many instructional models available that students and teachers should never be bored with teaching or learning. Following are some instructional options:

- **Differentiated instruction** provides students with learning opportunities that hook into their personal interests, cognitive levels, previous experiences, and learning modalities (Tomlinson, 1999). Differentiation does not mean ability grouping, tracking, or retention. Research has shown that these practices are counterproductive (Good & Brophy, 1997; Barr & Parrett, 2003).

- **Problem-based learning and inquiry learning** begin with an issue or a problem that does not have a pat answer or simple solution (Burke, 1999). This type of instruction requires an extended time format that allows for ample research and group discussion. Problem-based and inquiry learning link learning to the real world (Ronis, 2001).

- **Service learning** links content to a project that has an observable impact on the school or community. Because service learning connects students to real-world learning activities, this type of learning helps students remember what they have learned, retain more, and grow more connections in their brains (Diamond, 1988). Service learning is an effective strategy for reducing school dropout rates, and it provides benefits to the school and community (Barr & Parrett, 2003).

- **Socratic seminar** is built upon the practice of the Greek philosopher and teacher Socrates. This type of instruction requires the teacher to guide students rather than lecture students. Teachers facilitate learning though a series of questions.

This is only a partial list of modern models of teaching. (For more ideas refer to *Models of Teaching* [Joyce, Weil, & Calhoun, 2004] and *Dimensions of Learning* [Marzano & Pickering, 1997].) You may adapt and modify these models or you may choose other models that suit you and your students' needs.

To complement the models above, you may employ best practices within the models. Figure 1.6 lists some best practices commonly found in the classroom. When implementing instructional models, choose one or more of these best practices to enhance your instruction. Selecting strategies that strongly support the model saves time and increases the effectiveness of the model (Williams & Dunn, 2000).

| FIGURE 1.6 | **Best Practices: Making a Difference** |

- **Multiple Intelligences.** Howard Gardner (1983, 1993) identified eight intelligences: verbal/linguistic, logical/mathematic, visual/spatial, musical/rhythmic, bodily/kinesthetic, interpersonal, intrapersonal, and naturalist. Some students have more bodily/kinesthetic intelligence, while others have more naturalist intelligence. Be sure your instruction builds on your students' intelligences. Provide activities for each of the intelligences as often as possible.

- **Emotional Intelligence.** Goleman (1995, p. xiv) explains that "human competencies such as self-awareness, self-control, and empathy" as well as problem solving, listening, conflict resolution, and cooperation are often more indicative of a person's potential for lifelong success than a person's IQ. Take time to foster students' emotional intelligence in your lessons.

- **Graphic Organizers.** These visual tools help students organize and process information. Graphic organizers encourage students to make connections and discern relationships. Use graphic organizers to discover what and how students are thinking and to assess whether or not students are learning.

- **Technology.** While nothing can take the place of human interaction, computer technology offers many advantages for all learners. Computer learning is self-paced and interactive. Use computer learning to tap into students' natural affinity for technology while bolstering the technology skills they need for everyday life (Tapscott, 1999).

- **Learning Centers.** Learning centers allow students to perform tasks in order to master certain skills or increase their understanding of specific content. Provide ample time for students to use learning centers outside of whole group instruction.

- **Cooperative Learning Structures.** Cooperative learning puts students at the center of the learning process and increases student motivation. Cooperative learning fosters positive interdependence, individual accountability, group processing, face-to-face interaction, and collaboration (Johnson, Johnson, & Holubec, 1986). Be sure to include cooperative activities in your instruction.

- **Brain-Compatible Learning Strategies.** Discoveries in neuroscience have affirmed that learning is enhanced when instruction includes active participation, metacognitive activities, risk taking, social interaction and cooperation, and emotional, intellectual, and physical connections to content. Take care to design your instruction so that it correlates with how the brain works.

Instructional decision making is not about turning to a certain page in the textbook, reading the text, and completing the problems on the next page. The challenge is to select instructional models and strategies as if selecting the finest grapes to make the finest wine. Take time to choose the instructional model and strategies that will engage students in active learning.

ASSESSMENT

After choosing curricular and instructional approaches, the next step is to design assessment. It is essential that not only the curriculum and instruction be well planned but also that the assessment align with the curriculum and instruction for the learning experience to be complete.

Student performance is assessed "to improve education, determine success, and communicate results" (Carr & Harris, 2001, p. 64). Assessment happens during every phase of the teaching-learning process: before, during, and after teaching.

Assessment Before Teaching

The key question for this phase of assessment is: What do students already know about what teachers are about to teach them? Research suggests that students learn new information best when they connect new information to prior knowledge (Wolfe, 2001). Teachers can use the following tools to awaken students' prior knowledge.

KWL

Complete a KWL as a class. Donna Ogle (1986) created the KWL to help teachers assess what students already know about a subject, what they want to learn, and what they have learned after the lesson. See Figure 1.7 for a sample KWL.

FIGURE 1.7	KWL

What I Know	What I Want to Learn	What I Learned

Note: The KWL strategy was developed by Donna Ogle.

Pointed Questions

Ask pointed questions that reveal students' understanding and misunderstandings about a topic. Use questions to prompt a class discussion or individual journal writing. For example, before watching a video about slavery, you might ask students: When have you been treated unfairly? What did it feel like? How did you handle the situation? Have you ever seen others being treated unfairly? You might return to the questions after the video to help students understand how the slaves might have felt.

Brainstorm

Challenge students to list words that come to mind when you mention a certain topic or term related to a topic. Ask students to discuss their ideas with the class or write their ideas in their journals. For example, if you were beginning a unit on the Civil War, you might ask students to list words they associate with the Civil War.

Assessment During Teaching

The key questions for this phase of assessment are: Are students understanding the content? Are they with me? Should I move ahead, slow down, back up, or connect to past learning? Will they be ready for the final performance or project? Assessment at this phase of learning should be formative; that is, it should gauge how well students are learning and what adjustments should be made in teaching.

Formative assessments focus on whether or not the students are beginning to connect, organize, classify, and categorize the content. Tools for helping gauge whether the content is taking hold include

- concept webs,
- mind maps,
- Venn diagrams, and
- analogy or simile charts.

Formative assessments also measure how well students are measuring up to the standards. Tools for measuring student learning in accordance with standards include

- learning games,
- short-answer responses,

- quizzes,

- essays,

- partial unit tests,

- activities,

- performances,

- small projects,

- graphic organizers, and

- outlines.

Teachers can use any of the above tools to determine how well their students are learning and how they might adjust your instruction in order to be more effective.

Assessment After Teaching

The key questions for this phase of assessment are: How will students show what they know? How will I engineer a comprehensive assessment that provides evidence of the mastery of required standards? What will I do to provide empirical data about the dynamics of the learning situation and the effectiveness of my teaching? Assessment at this phase of learning should be summative; that is, it summarizes what the students have learned. It is typically used to evaluate the degree to which students have understood the material and the effectiveness of a lesson or unit. Summative assessments include

- performance tasks,

- checklists, and

- rubrics.

Performance Tasks

Performance tasks are projects that are used to assess learning. Performance tasks are challenging, are often real-world related, and typically have more than one solution. Performance tasks can be designed to incorporate both standards and curriculum, and they appeal to various types of learners. According to Lewin and Shoemaker (1998), a performance task has the following characteristics:

- Students have some choice in selecting the task.

- The task requires students to expand upon core knowledge content and the use of specific processes.

- The task has an explicit scoring system.

- The task has value outside the classroom (i.e., real-world application).

- The task is crafted to measure what it purports to measure.

Performance tasks can be created in a variety of ways. Examples of performance tasks for various subjects are found in chapter 2.

Performance tasks are measured by performance assessments. According to Popham (1999), performance assessments should meet the following criteria:

- Performance assessments should use *multiple evaluative criteria.* Students' performances should be judged using more than one criterion.

- Performance assessments should *prespecify quality standards.* Teachers should clearly explain the criteria upon which the students' performances will be judged prior to judging the performances.

- Performance assessments should use *human judgments* rather than electronic scoring devices to determine how successful a student's performance really is.

Checklists and rubrics fit the criteria described above and are ideal for assessing performance tasks.

Checklists

Checklists can be used to evaluate performance tasks or other projects and products. Checklists provide measurable categories and indicators for judging products and performances. Teachers can use checklists to give students in-depth feedback on their learning. Students can use checklists to judge their performances or products and to ensure that they measure up to various levels of achievement. Checklists have the following characteristics:

- Checklists are very flexible.

- Checklists can be used with authentic assessments that have multiple components.

- Checklists address multiple facets of a single unit or several units.

- Checklists often include student self-assessments.

- Checklists can incorporate rating scales.

- Checklists are aligned with standards.

- Checklists provide accurate records of achievement for student portfolios.

- Checklists communicate clear expectations at the beginning of the unit. Students can use checklists as roadmaps while working on their projects.

Checklists can be created in a variety of ways. More information and examples of checklists are found in chapter 3.

Rubrics

Rubrics can be used to score performances, products, and projects. Rubrics provide teachers, students, and parents with a clear picture of what students know and are able to do, as well as the levels to which students demonstrate their knowledge (Depka, 2001). Through rubrics, teachers define criteria (linked to standards) and indicators (linked to performance levels). Clearly defining criteria and indicators helps students realize that they can achieve learning goals (Schmoker, 1996). See chapter 4 for tips on how to create rubrics.

— ■ —

Curriculum, instruction, and assessment are the cornerstones of teaching and learning. The remainder of this book focuses primarily on assessment and the three avenues to authentic assessment—performance tasks, checklists, and rubrics.

CHAPTER 2

Performance Tasks

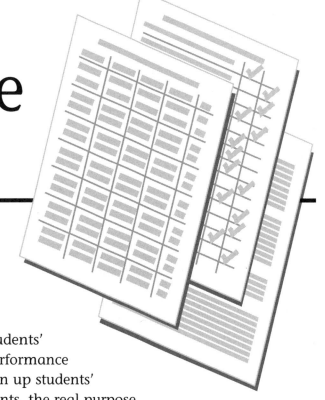

WHAT ARE PERFORMANCE TASKS?

Performance tasks are activities that measure students'
mastery of real-world concepts and processes. Performance
tasks are not merely fun activities created to liven up students'
learning. While they may be enjoyable for students, the real purpose
of performance tasks is to measure student learning of particular
concepts and processes. According to Lewin and Shoemaker (1998, p. 5),
a performance task has the following characteristics:

- Students have some choice in selecting the task.

- The task requires students to expand upon core knowledge content
  and use specific processes.

- The task has an explicit scoring system.

- The task has value outside the classroom; that is, it can be applied to
  a real-world situation.

- The task is carefully crafted to measure what it purports to measure.

Selecting or Creating the Performance Task

How does the teacher choose a performance task? Figure 2.1 lists a series
of questions that should be considered when selecting or creating a performance task. Not all performance tasks will satisfy all seven criteria, but
teachers should strive to meet at least five of the seven criteria.

FIGURE 2.1   **Evaluative Criteria for Performance Tasks**

- ■ **Generalizability.** Is it highly likely that students' performance on the task will generalize to comparable tasks?

- ■ **Authenticity.** Is the task similar to what students might encounter in the real world as opposed to only in school?

- ■ **Multiple foci.** Does the task measure multiple instructional outcomes instead of only one?

- ■ **Teachability.** Is the task one that students can become more proficient in as a result of a teacher's instruction?

- ■ **Fairness.** Is the task fair to all students? (Does the task avoid bias based on personal characteristics such as students' gender, ethnicity, or socioeconomic status?)

- ■ **Feasibility.** Is it realistic to implement the task in relation to its cost, space, time, and equipment requirements?

- ■ **Scorability.** Is the task likely to elicit student responses that can be reliably and accurately evaluated?

Adapted from Popham, W. J. (1999). *Classroom assessment: What teachers need to know* (p. 165). Needham Heights, MA: Allyn and Bacon. Copyright © 1999 by Allyn and Bacon. Reprinted by permission.

When selecting or creating performance tasks, teachers should also give students some flexibility in choosing the performance task (Lewin Shoemaker, 1998). For example, if the teacher has crafted a performance task about geometry, he or she may allow one group of students to draw and label geometric shapes, another group to write a story using at least five geometric shapes, a third group to make a presentation of geometric shapes used in the workplace, etc.

Expanding Content Knowledge and Using Specific Processes

Performance tasks must be created with an end in mind: expanding content knowledge and mastering specific processes. Teachers should choose specific content and process standards and build a performance task that fosters students' meeting of these standards.

Explicit Scoring System

Performance tasks must be measurable if they are to be useful for student assessment. Teachers should create an explicit scoring system for the performance task and share this system with students as they are introduced to the task. Students must know what is expected of them before they begin the task.

Applicable to the Real World

One of the most important characteristics of a performance task is its applicability to the real world. Teachers must answer students' perennial question: But how can I use this in my life? Performance tasks that help students discover answers to real-world dilemmas not only expand students' knowledge, they remind students that their learning matters because it touches their lives.

Task Measures What It Purports to Measure

Finally, the performance task must be designed so that it accurately measures what it sets out to measure. Performance tasks are not merely busywork or forms of entertainment. It is not enough for students to create a finished product if that product does not specifically address the content and process standards outlined by the teacher. Performance tasks must measure students' content and process knowledge in relation to specific standards.

HOW TO CREATE PERFORMANCE TASKS

As with all instructional design, it is best to plan a performance task with the end in mind. Wiggins and McTighe (1998) call this backward planning. Burke's (1999) performance task template uses the backward planning model. Her model designates the following steps in creating a performance task:

- Choose learning standards

- Write a task description

- Plan for direct, whole-class instruction

- Create options for group work

- Include individual work

- Designate assessment methods

For a sample template, see the Examples section at the end of this chapter. You may use the template when creating your own performance assessments. Sample performance tasks for elementary, middle, and high school are also shown in the Examples section at the end of this chapter.

Choose Learning Standards

You should begin planning your performance task by asking: What do I want my students to know and be able to do when they complete this task? The best way to answer this question is to name the standards that you wish students to meet. Establishing the goal before starting the task is essential to planning a successful performance task.

The Elementary School Performance Task (see the Examples section at the end of this chapter) shows a sample performance task for kindergarten. Notice that the task designates several standards in both mathematics and language arts. When you are designing your performance task, consider choosing learning standards from two or more content areas.

Write a Task Description

After you have determined what learning standards you will target, take time to brainstorm possible learning tasks that allow students to demonstrate their ability to meet the learning standards. For example, if one of the standards is "students begin to write and draw pictures for specific purposes and for a specific audience," be sure to include writing and drawing as part of the learning task.

Plan for Direct, Whole-Class Instruction

Direct instruction is an important component of performance assessments. Considering your learning standards and your task description, ask yourself:

- What information do students need to complete the task?

- What types of direct instruction will help students gain that knowledge?

Bear in mind that students can receive direct instruction from someone other than their teacher. Consider inviting guest speakers to class, showing videos/DVDs about the topic, asking experts to explain how to do certain tasks (e.g., ask a graphic designer to show students how to use Adobe Illustrator), leading whole-class discussions on a topic, etc. (See Examples section at the end of this chapter for other samples of direct instruction methods.) One powerful way to connect performance tasks to real-world tasks is by allowing students to receive instruction from sources outside the classroom.

Create Options for Group Work

Group work is an essential component of performance tasks. First, group work challenges students to cooperate with others. Cooperation is an essential life skill that ties performance tasks to the real world. Second, group work allows students to make choices in the learning. Allowing students to choose from several group work options ensures that students remain interested in the performance task. Third, group work encourages students to create a product or performance that shows what they know and are able to do. When students discover all they know and all they can do, they become excited about their learning and often seek to further that learning.

When creating options for group work, keep these components in mind. Be sure to devise tasks that promote cooperation. Devise methods for monitoring group work and ensuring that students cooperate with one another. Create real options for students. Allow them to choose between many types of tasks (e.g., drawing, writing, singing or dancing, building, speaking, researching, etc.). Create group work tasks that allow students' abilities to blossom.

Include Individual Work

Performance tasks must include individual work to ensure that each student understands and can apply the information learned through direct instruction and group work. Design individual tasks that allow students to synthesize all they have learned in the performance task. Remember to align the task with the standards you have set for the performance task. Ask yourself if the individual work shows what each student knows and is able to do in relation to the prescribed standards.

Designate Assessment Methods

Performance task assessments may include traditional components (e.g., multiple-choice test), checklists, and rubrics. (For more information on checklists and rubrics, see chapters 3 and 4.) Whatever methods you choose, be sure to devise assessments for each component of the task. That is, you should assess what students learned during direct instruction, group work, and individual work.

Assessments may be formative or summative. Use formative assessments throughout the tasks to check students' understanding and make adjustments to instruction or tasks as needed. These formative assessments need not be graded. Use summative assessments to determine what students learned and were able to do. These summative assessments should be scored or graded according to learning standards.

Popham (1999, p. 5) suggests that performance task assessments include these features:

- **Multiple evaluative criteria.** Judge students' performances using more than one criteria.

- **Prespecified quality standards.** Clearly explain the quality standards to students before students are evaluated. (Lewin and Shoemaker [1998, p. 29] suggest that you show samples of past student work that meets the standards.)

- **Judgmental appraisal.** Use human judgments, rather than electronic scoring devices, to evaluate students' performance.

Aim to include all three features in your assessment methods. Finally, be sure to show students samples of work that meets the standards.

Review the Performance Task

Before you unleash the performance task on your students, take time to review it. Be sure that the task allows students to demonstrate their ability to meet the designated learning standards. Check that direct instruction, group work, and individual work all contribute to meeting the learning standards. Be sure that the assessments judge students' performances in light of the learning standards.

— ■ —

In the next two chapters, you will learn how to create and use checklists and rubrics to evaluate student work. These methods can be used in conjunction with or separately from performance tasks. However, all three are essential components of a well-rounded assessment program.

Examples

Following is a performance task template teachers can use to create their own performance task, plus sample performance tasks for projects for elementary, middle, and high school students. These performance tasks correspond to the sample checklists and rubrics for the equivalent grade levels provided in chapters 3 and 4.

The appendices contain additional samples of assessment tools teachers can review and customize with their own ideas or projects.

▪ PERFORMANCE TASK TEMPLATE ▪

COURSE/CLASS _____ GRADE _____

STANDARDS

TASK DESCRIPTION

DIRECT INSTRUCTION FOR WHOLE CLASS | The whole class will be involved in the following learning experience:

GROUP WORK

Group One	Group Two	Group Three	Group Four	Group Five

INDIVIDUAL WORK

METHODS OF ASSESSMENT

Adapted from Burke, K. (1999). *The mindful school: How to assess authentic learning* (p. 91). Arlington Heights, IL: SkyLight Training and Publishing. Used with permission.

▪ ELEMENTARY PERFORMANCE TASK ▪

COURSE/CLASS _Writing and math_   **GRADE** _Kindergarten_

STANDARDS _Mathematics. Geometry standard: Students identify common objects around them and describe their geometric features and position. Language Arts. Standard 4 for writing process: Students discuss ideas and stories for someone to write. Students use pictures, letters, and words to write. Standard 5 for writing process: Students begin to write and draw pictures for specific purposes and specific audiences._

TASK DESCRIPTION

Attention all kindergarten students: You have been selected by the principal to create and star in the Shapes All Around Us Show. The show, which features the eight basic shapes, will be performed for the preschoolers on April 15. Your group will take part in the show by creating an invitation, a shape display, a poster, or a big book of shapes.

DIRECT INSTRUCTION FOR WHOLE CLASS | The whole class will be involved in the following learning experience:

1. Students will listen to and discuss shape books.
2. Students will locate shapes within the school environment by taking an "environmental walk" around the school.
3. Teacher will demonstrate differences between the eight shapes using models, songs, and/or poems. (The eight shapes are circle, square, oval, rectangle, diamond, heart, triangle, and star.)
4. Teacher will model appropriate social skills for group work. Students will work in small cooperative learning groups to sort and compare shapes.

GROUP WORK

Group One	Group Two	Group Three	Group Four
Create an invitation for the preschool class to attend the Shapes All Around Us Show. Ask each student in the class to sign the card using their first and last names.	Create large model shapes to use in the demonstration part of the Shapes All Around Us Show. Be sure to include all eight shapes—circle, square, oval, rectangle, diamond, heart, triangle, and star.	Make one poster for each of the eight shapes—circle, square, oval, rectangle, diamond, heart, triangle, and star. Use magazine clippings, digital or conventional pictures, and drawings of shapes found in our environment. You will use the posters during the Shapes All Around Us Show.	Make a big book that includes all of the shapes—circle, square, oval, rectangle, diamond, heart, triangle, and star. You will present the book to the preschool class after the Shapes All Around Us Show.

INDIVIDUAL WORK

1. Create an eight-page book; each page of the book will feature one of the eight shapes—circle, square, oval, rectangle, diamond, heart, triangle, or star. Students can use magazine clippings, digital or conventional pictures, and drawings of shapes found in the environment.
2. Write and/or draw journal reflections about what you learned.
3. Identify each shape by name.
4. Sign the invitation to the preschool class, using both your first and last names. Make sure your handwriting is neat and legible.

METHODS OF ASSESSMENT

1. Checklist for individual interviews to determine whether or not students can identify each shape
2. Checklist to assess each group's project
3. Checklist to assess journal reflections
4. Rubric to assess each student's eight-page book

Thank you to Jenni LaMar (Lebanon Community Schools, Indiana) and Linda Snyder (Center Grove Community Schools, Indiana) for providing the ideas for this performance task.

▪ MIDDLE SCHOOL PERFORMANCE TASK ▪

COURSE/CLASS ___Social Studies___ GRADE ___6___

STANDARDS* 6.3.1: Explain the components of most maps (title, scale, legend, grid, and projection). Compare different map types (topographic, thematic, etc.) and different map projections, and explain the appropriate use for each. 6.3.3: Identify the names and locations of countries and major cities in Europe and the Western Hemisphere. Identify the states of Mexico and the provinces of Canada. 6.3.4: Describe major physical characteristics (natural features, such as land and water forms, climate, natural vegetation, and native wildlife) of regions in Europe and the Americas. 6.3.5: Describe major cultural characteristics (human features, such as population characteristics, communication and transportation networks, religion and customs, and how people make a living or build homes and other structures) of regions in Europe and the Western Hemisphere. 6.3.10: Compare and contrast cultural patterns—such as language, religion, and ethnicity—in various parts of Europe; the Caribbean; and North, South, and Central America. 6.5.7: Examine art, music, literature, and architecture in Europe and the Americas; explain their relationship to the societies that created them; and give examples of how artistic ideas have spread from one culture to another. 6.5.8: Use a variety of resources, including newspapers, magazines, Web sites, and databases, to collect and analyze data on cultural factors in countries of Europe and the Americas. Use charts, graphs, and other data to compare and hypothesize the relation of these factors to a nation's development.

TASK DESCRIPTION

Because of your extensive knowledge about Latin America, you have been asked to create a proposal for a school-sponsored spring break trip to Latin America. Your trip should include popular tourist sites, historical landmarks, culture of the area, interesting or unique landmarks, and a map of your travel route. You will present your proposal to the school board on March 29 in order for your spring break plans to be adopted for the next school year.

DIRECT INSTRUCTION FOR WHOLE CLASS   The whole class will be involved in the following learning experience:

1. Examine maps of each region of Latin America.
2. Listen to guest speakers from each region of Latin America.
3. View a PowerPoint presentation by the teacher on Latin America.
4. Read the textbook and take notes.

GROUP WORK

Group One	Group Two	Group Three	Group Four	Group Five
Conduct research about Mexico. Make a proposal for visiting this region on spring break. Your trip should include popular tourist sites, historical landmarks, culture of the area, interesting or unique landforms, and a map of your travel route.	Conduct research about Central America: Belize, Costa Rica, El Salvador, Guatemala, Honduras, Nicaragua, and Panama. Make a proposal for visiting this region on spring break. Your trip should include popular tourist sites, historical landmarks, culture of the area, interesting or unique landforms, and a map of your travel route.	Conduct research about the Caribbean region: Bahamas, Cuba, Dominican Republic, Haiti, Jamaica, Puerto Rico, Trinidad and Tobago, and Virgin Islands. Make a proposal for visiting this region on spring break. Your trip should include popular tourist sites, historical landmarks, culture of the area, interesting or unique landforms, and a map of your travel route.	Conduct research about Brazil, Paraguay, Argentina, and Uruguay. Make a proposal for visiting this region on spring break. Your trip should include popular tourist sites, historical landmarks, culture of the area, interesting or unique landforms, and a map of your travel route.	Conduct research about the Andes region: Bolivia, Chile, Colombia, Ecuador, Peru, and Venezuela. Make a proposal for visiting this region on spring break. Your trip should include popular tourist sites, historical landmarks, culture of the area, interesting or unique landforms, and a map of your travel route.

INDIVIDUAL WORK

1. Design a travel poster for your assigned region.
2. Devise a slogan that promotes your region and entices people to visit your region.
3. Create a collage that represents what you learned about your region.

METHODS OF ASSESSMENT

1. Rubric to assess each group's proposal
2. Checklist for travel poster and slogan
3. Rubric to assess collage
4. Map test

Thank you to Leslie Henegar (Lebanon Middle School, Lebanon Community Schools, Indiana) for providing the ideas for this performance task. (*Standards from Indiana Department of Education. [n.d.]. Indiana academic standards. Retrieved March 8, 2004, from http://www.indianastandards.org/)

■ HIGH SCHOOL PERFORMANCE TASK ■

COURSE/CLASS __Chemistry__ GRADE _High School_

STANDARDS*

C.1.41: Describe the role of light, heat, and electrical energies in physical, chemical, and nuclear changes.

C.1.42: Describe that the energy release per gram of material is much larger in nuclear fusion or fission reactions than in chemical reactions. The change in mass (calculated by $E=mc^2$) is small but significant in nuclear reactions.

C.1.43: Calculate the amount of radioactive substance remaining after an integral number of half-lives have passed.

TASK DESCRIPTION

A power company is considering using nuclear power in the Indianapolis area to increase its supply of available electricity to local residents. The CEO has asked you to write a report outlining the impact that a nuclear power plant would have on the community. You will present your preliminary PowerPoint presentation to the board of directors and submit your final report to the power company.

DIRECT INSTRUCTION FOR WHOLE CLASS | The whole class will be involved in the following learning experience:

1. Watch the PBS presentation Meltdown at Three Mile Island.
2. Receive instruction on writing nuclear equations and calculating half-life for various radioactive isotopes, including those used in nuclear power plants.
3. Perform a lab experiment on the effect of distance and shielding on radioactive particles.
4. Complete a lab experiment to determine the half-life of radioactive isotopes.

GROUP WORK

Group One	Group Two	Group Three	Group Four	Group Five
Create and present a PowerPoint presentation that illustrates the health risks posed by nuclear energy.	Create and present a PowerPoint presentation that explains alternatives to nuclear energy.	Create and present a PowerPoint presentation that describes how a nuclear power plant works.	Create and present a PowerPoint presentation that describes three possible sites on which to build a plant.	Create and present a PowerPoint presentation that recommends methods for disposing of nuclear waste.

INDIVIDUAL WORK

Write a report to the power company. Include the following information that you learned from the group presentations:

• Describe how a nuclear power plant converts fuel sources into electricity. Be sure to explain how the nuclear reaction takes place.

• Tell how to dispose of nuclear waste. Estimate how much waste will be produced each year and how long the waste must decay before it is considered safe.

• Describe the potential health risks for those who live near the plant.

• Tell about the proposed site for the plant. Include population data within a 5-, 10-, 15-, 20-, and 25-mile radius.

• Create a proposal for using an alternative energy source to generate electricity.

METHODS OF ASSESSMENT

1. Checklist for lab experiment on the effect of distance and shielding on radioactive particles
2. Rubric for a lab report on the the half-life of radioactive isotopes
3. Checklist for each group's PowerPoint presentation
4. Rubric for individual reports

Thank you to Cathy Glick (Hamilton Southeastern High School, Hamilton Southeastern Schools, Indiana) for providing the ideas for this performance task. (*Standards from Indiana Department of Education. [n.d.]. Indiana academic standards. Retrieved March 8, 2004, from http://www.indianastandards.org/)

CHAPTER 3

Checklists

Imagine an Olympic ice-skating competition. The graceful skaters put years of practice to the test. They perform at the pinnacle of their craft and then sit breathless awaiting the judges' decision.

For those of us on the edge of our seats at home, we arbitrarily judge the performance—we either like it or don't like it. We know that if a skater falls while attempting a jump, he or she will be penalized. But we don't understand the point system well enough to predict the judges' marks. The judges, on the other hand, do understand the point system and have spent many years judging the sport. Still, judges' scores may vary widely. Watching this competition and the method of scoring helps us realize why it is so important to develop fair and unbiased assessment tools.

Checklists and rubrics are two forms of assessment that attempt to precisely measure students' performance and projects. This chapter focuses on checklists and the next chapter focuses on rubrics.

RATING SCALE

The rating scale is the basis for both checklists and rubrics. Rating scales give precise indicators of achievement. For example, if we used a rating scale to judge an Olympic ice-skating competition, every judge would know exactly what criteria to look for and would use these criteria objectively rather than arbitrarily. Precision is a hallmark of rating scales, whether they measure performance on a scale from 0 to 3, 1 to 5, or 0 to 10.

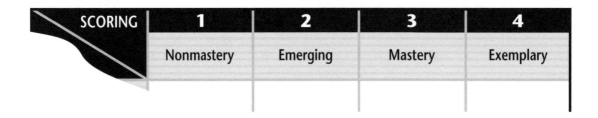

FIGURE 3.1   Rating Scale

SCORING	1	2	3	4
	Nonmastery	Emerging	Mastery	Exemplary

The rating scale usually appears at the top of a checklist or rubric (see Figure 3.1). Some scales are simple; for example, 0 = task incomplete and 1 = task complete. Others are more complex; for example, 1 = nonmastery, 2 = emerging mastery, 3 = mastery, and 4 = exemplary. The scale can be used as a formative assessment (e.g., a checklist for students to use while working on a project) or as a summative assessment (as part of a rubric the teacher uses to assess students' final projects).

Let's look at an example. Imagine that students are working on a multi-faceted project and an early benchmark in the project is a computer-generated graph. Students must complete the graph before the final project is due. You might choose to create a rating scale for the graph that will help students determine whether or not they are on track with the project. The rating scale can provide necessary guidelines and feedback that students need in order to proceed with the project.

You might use a scale such as the one shown in Figure 3.2 to rate the students' work so far. In this case, the scale would be formative; it would be used to correct the students' work before they are so far into the project that they can no longer recover from early mistakes. You might do a quick evaluation of each student's graph, highlighting or circling the appropriate column. The student could use the information to amend his or her graph and continue to work on the final project.

If you are working with preschool or elementary school students, consider using pictorial rating scales. Nonreaders can understand the pictures more readily. Figure 3.3 shows several sample pictorial scales. Pictorial scales can be used for checklists and rubrics.

Two of the biggest advantages of rating scales are that they take little time and use few resources. For example, you might reproduce a rating scale on a half sheet of paper, highlight the appropriate rating, write comments

FIGURE 3.2 **Sample Rating Scale for Computer-Generated Graph**

SCORING / CRITERIA	1 Start Over	2 Needs Work	3 Almost There	4 Mastery (You got it!)	5 Exemplary (Great work!)
	Inaccurate	Some inaccuracies	Effective overall	Effective and accurate	A great model
	Poor technical execution	Poor technical execution	Sharpen the technical execution	Good technical execution	Great technical execution
	Hard to read	Needs more time and work	Needs more attention to detail	Graphic tells the story	Mastery of the concept
	Check the facts	Start-up is okay, but keep going			Graphic tells the story

FIGURE 3.3 **Pictorial Rating Scales**

Sample Scales

 Try Again!    Doing Better!    You Did It!

 You're on the Rise!  You're Beginning to Shine!  You'r Work Is Ablaze!

Tips for Pictorial Scales
- A picture is worth a thousand words!
- Use story characters, cartoons, and animal pictures that students like (see examples at right).
- Use pictorial checklists to help students understand what is required of them (i.e., standards).

Jerry Giraffe
Stretch your skills—I'll help you!

Penelope Porcupine
Still rough on the edges—needs some work.

Wally Warthog
You "hogged" loads of good things in your work.

Norman the Buffalo
Your work is a huge stampeding success!

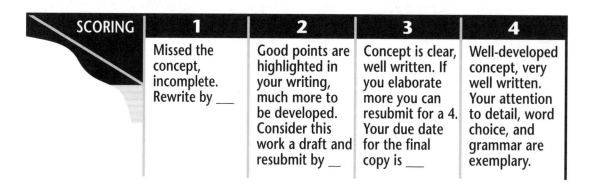

FIGURE 3.4   Rating Scale with Comments

SCORING	1	2	3	4
	Missed the concept, incomplete. Rewrite by ___	Good points are highlighted in your writing, much more to be developed. Consider this work a draft and resubmit by ___	Concept is clear, well written. If you elaborate more you can resubmit for a 4. Your due date for the final copy is ___	Well-developed concept, very well written. Your attention to detail, word choice, and grammar are exemplary.

below the scale, attach the rating to the students' project, and return the project to the student. An example rating scale with room for comments is shown in Figure 3.4.

Rating scales are a quick and effective means of assessment:

- Rating scales provide a mental orientation to criterion-based rating, the premise of the checklist and rubric.

- Rating scales are authentic benchmarks as opposed to worksheets that may or may not align with the summative evaluation.

- Rating scales provide objective, quantifiable, specific feedback to students that they can use to refine their work and heighten their chance of success.

- Rating scales encourage metacognition and reflection; students must think about their work and evaluate their progress before proceeding to the next step.

WHAT ARE CHECKLISTS?

Checklists are an in-depth version of a rating scale. Checklists provide a measurable list of categories and indicators for projects, products, or performances. Checklists allow students to judge their performances, projects, or products to make sure they have achieved the highest possible rating in each category. Every checklist includes these components:

- Rating scale

- Criteria that reflect standards

- Multiple indicators that reflect level of performance

- Grading scale

Figure 3.5 features a checklist template. (For a blank template you can use to create your own checklist, see Examples at the end of this chapter.) The first row comprises the rating scale. The left column features the criteria and multiple indicators. At the bottom of the checklist is a grading scale.

FIGURE 3.5   Checklist Template

■ CRITERIA CHECKLIST ■

COURSE/CLASS _____ GRADE _____
STANDARDS _____
ACTIVITY _____

CRITERIA/PERFORMANCE INDICATORS	Not Yet [0]	Some Evidence [1]
Criterion		
• Indicator		
• Indicator		
• Indicator		
Criterion		
• Indicator		
• Indicator		
• Indicator		
Criterion		
• Indicator		
• Indicator		
• Indicator		
Criterion		
• Indicator		
• Indicator		
• Indicator		

COMMENTS

Grading Scale
____points = A
____points = B
____points = C
____points = D
____points = F

HOW TO CREATE CHECKLISTS

Preplanning for Checklists

The key to setting up a checklist is to match the checklist to the standards and outcomes targeted for the project, product, or performance. Teachers can begin by listing standards, curriculum, and instructional targets, and follow up by determining how students will demonstrate what they have learned in a summative assessment. Teachers can use this process to abandon frivolous content and to hone in on critical instructional components.

List standards, curriculum goals, and instructional targets. Take time to organize your thoughts in a chart with these categories: need to know, nice to know, and where to go (see Figure 3.6). Write critical standards and goals in the first column. List meaningful instructional targets in the second column. Before filling in the third column, ask yourself how you and your students might find time to accomplish the items in the first two columns. List resources you and your students might use to get more information in the third column.

This chart is very simple, but it may be your most critical planning tool for ensuring focus in the unit. It is a structured, linear organizer, rather than a thematic web organizer. It is important to use linear planning, because it helps you avoid falling into extraneous content or activities that are not directly aligned with the standards, objectives, and assessments. (However, you might choose to use the ideas in the Where to Go column to add enrichment activities to the unit.)

Determine how students will demonstrate what they have learned in a summative assessment. You may choose to combine a test or quiz with one or more authentic means of assessment. For example, you might ask students to write a report, do a speech, or create a work of art. Whatever method(s) you choose, be sure you answer these questions when creating the assessment:

- How will students demonstrate what they have learned from the Need to Know column?

- How will students demonstrate what they have learned from the Nice to Know column? How will they transfer this knowledge to other content areas or other situations so that they might retain knowledge and use it in the future?

- How will students show that they know Where to Go? In other words, how might they demonstrate their technical abilities? (Remember, in our technologically savvy society, students need to know how to research, analyze, discern, and use the Internet and other technological tools.)

FIGURE 3.6 **Instructional Component List**

■ GRAPHIC ORGANIZER FOR FOCUSING THE UNIT ■

NEED TO KNOW	NICE TO KNOW	WHERE TO GO
■ National standards ■ National content-specific standards ■ State standards ■ Proficiencies ■ Local curriculum maps or guides	■ Good auxiliary information that adds meaning to the content for students ■ Content integrated from other content areas that makes content transferable and more real-world ■ Motivational information that is local, is age appropriate, and sparks inquiry and curiosity in students ■ Stories that aid in visualization and retention ■ Current events and issues that hinge on the content and are presented in as timely a manner as possible	■ Internet sites ■ Books ■ Reference materials ■ Local experts ■ National experts ■ Organizations ■ Community interest groups ■ Career connections ■ Further study resources ■ Other interested students (perhaps in upper grades)

All items on the graphic organizer should be assessed at some point in the unit. Some will be evaluated in the summative assessment, and others will be evaluated in formative assessments along the way.

For example, you might assess students' technical skills early in the unit so that students can make corrections to their work and successfully work toward the completion of the unit. If students are working on a research project, you might assess students' Internet resources near the beginning of the unit so that students can correct or enhance their research. This will not only help students remain on target, it will also save you time during the summative assessment, because you will not need to reassess the resources. Students then use the Internet resources to create their demonstration speech (the final product) and you evaluate them with a summative assessment.

As you develop the summative assessment, take time to picture what an exemplary ("A") project might look like and might include. Be sure to include those characteristics in your checklist. The next section provides step-by-step instructions for creating a checklist.

Steps for Creating Checklists

Step 1: Create a Rating Scale

Most checklists use a very simple 0 to 1 scale; 0 represents not yet and 1 represents some evidence. Remember, if you are teaching preschool or elementary students, you may create a pictorial scale. Figure 3.7 shows a sample rating scale for a summative checklist.

FIGURE 3.7   Sample Rating Scale for Checklist

■ CRITERIA CHECKLIST ■		
COURSE/CLASS _____		GRADE ____
STANDARD _____		
ACTIVITY _____		
CRITERIA/PERFORMANCE INDICATORS	Not Yet [0]	Some Evidence [1]
Criterion		
● *Indicator*		

Step 2: Determine Criteria and Performance Indicators

List the standards or critical learning to be evidenced in the assessment as criteria (broad categories) followed by indicators (specific categories). For an example, see Figure 3.8. "Use of Technology" is the criterion and the bulleted items are indicators. The figure shows an example of just one criterion with several indicators. To complete the checklist, be sure to include criteria and indicators for every standard you wish to assess.

FIGURE 3.8   Sample Criteria and Performance Indicators for Checklist

CRITERIA/PERFORMANCE INDICATORS	Not Yet [0]	Some Evidence [1]
Use of Technology		
● *Use six Internet sources.*		
● *Dialogue with a group from another school that is studying the same problem.*		
● *Use two other technology-driven research sites, such as organizational and governmental links.*		
● *Use presentation software to create visual aids for the final demonstration.*		
● *Construct your own graphic organizer to represent your data.*		

Checklists are helpful assessment tools because they do the following:

- Set clear expectations for students' projects, products, or performances

- Allow students to self-assess their progress

- Provide built-in list for students in the process of meeting expectations

- Provide feedback in a quick, easy-to-read format

- Show individualized data for each student, which is critical for decision making throughout a course or grade level

— ■ —

Checklists are an effective way for teachers and students alike to keep track of the performance indicators of a project. Checklists make grading easier for teachers and help students understand what is expected of them as they complete their products, performances, or projects.

Examples

Following are several checklists: a checklist template and sample checklists for elementary, middle, and high school levels. These checklists correspond to the sample performance tasks and rubrics for the equivalent grade levels provided in chapters 2 and 4. (See Appendix A for additional sample checklists.)

▪ CHECKLIST TEMPLATE ▪

COURSE/CLASS _____ GRADE _____

STANDARDS _____

_____

_____

ACTIVITY _____

CRITERIA/PERFORMANCE INDICATORS		Not Yet [0]	Some Evidence [1]
●			
●			
●			
●			
●			
●			
●			
●			
●			
●			
●			
●			
●			
●			
●			
●			
●			

COMMENTS

Grading Scale

____points = A   ____points = D
____points = B   ____points = F
____points = C

■ ELEMENTARY CHECKLIST ■

COURSE/CLASS _Writing and Math_   GRADE_Kindergarten_

STANDARDS _Language arts. Standard 4 for writing process: Students discuss ideas and stories for someone to write. Students use pictures, letters, and words to write. Standard 5 for writing process: Students begin to write and draw pictures for specific purposes and specific audiences._

ACTIVITY _Write and/or draw journal reflections about what you learned._

CRITERIA/PERFORMANCE INDICATORS	Not Yet [0]	Some Evidence [1]
Characteristics		
● Pictures of shapes		
● Names of shapes		
Organization		
● Moves from left to right		
● Moves from top to bottom		
● Puts in spaces		
● Uses punctuation		
● Uses capitalization		
Focus		
● Writes using pictures		
● Writes using letters		
● Writes using invented spelling		
● Writes words phonetically		
● Writes sentences		

COMMENTS

Grading Scale

11–12 points = A   7–8 points = D
10 points = B   0–6 points = F
9 points = C

Thank you to Jenni LaMar (Lebanon Middle School, Lebanon Community Schools, Indiana) and Linda Snyder (Center Grove Community Schools, Indiana) for providing the ideas for this checklist.

■ MIDDLE SCHOOL CHECKLIST ■

COURSE/CLASS _Social Studies_   **GRADE** _6_

STANDARDS* _6.3.5: Describe major cultural characteristics (human features, such as population characteristics, communication and transportation networks, religion and customs, and how people make a living or build homes and other structures) of Latin America. 6.3.10: Compare and contrast cultural patterns — such as language, religion, and ethnicity — in various parts of Latin America._

ACTIVITY _Create a collage that represents what your learned about your region._

CRITERIA/PERFORMANCE INDICATORS	Not Yet [0]	Some Evidence [1]
Work Habits		
• Gathers necessary supplies		
• Works independently		
• Asks for help when needed		
Use of Work Time		
• Does not give up quickly		
• Displays patience, takes time with work		
• Uses work time wisely		
• Cleans up work space		
Collage		
• Includes two examples of human figures		
• Includes two examples of religion		
• Includes two examples of buildings and architecture		
• Includes two examples of modes of transportation and communication		
• Includes two examples of leisure activities (sports, art, music, food)		
Presentation		
• Maintains eye contact with audience		
• Shows enthusiasm through voice inflection		
• Uses colorful and eye-catching props		
Reflection		
• Did you do what you were supposed to do?		
• Do you feel you know the key concepts about your region?		
• What would you do differently if you did this project again?		

COMMENTS

Grading Scale

_16–18_ points = A   _7–9_ points = D
_13–15_ points = B   _0–6_ points = F
_10–12_ points = C

Thank you to Leslie Henegar (Lebanon Middle School, Lebanon Community Schools, Indiana) for providing the ideas for this checklist. (*Standards from Indiana Department of Education. [n.d.]. _Indiana academic standards._ Retrieved March 8, 2004, from http://www.indianastandards.org/)

■ HIGH SCHOOL CHECKLIST 1 ■

COURSE/CLASS *Chemistry* _____ **GRADE** *High School*

STANDARDS* *C.1.41: Describe the role of light, heat, and electrical energies in physical, chemical, and nuclear changes.*
C.1.42: Describe that the energy release per gram of material is much larger in nuclear fusion or fission reactions than in chemical reactions. The change in mass (calculated by $E=mc^2$) is small but significant in nuclear reactions.
C.1.43: Calculate the amount of radioactive substance remaining after an integral number of half-lives have passed.

ACTIVITY *Create and present a PowerPoint presentation with your group (group 1: health risks; group 2: alternatives to nuclear energy; group 3: how a nuclear power plant works; group 4: three possible plant sites; group 5: nuclear waste disposal).*

CRITERIA/PERFORMANCE INDICATORS	Homer Simpson [0]	Albert Einstein [1]
Quality of Information		
● Accurate		
● Useful for writing final report		
● Related to group research topic		
● Provides insight into nuclear reactions and half-lives		
● Includes sources		
Group Dynamics		
● Participation by each member		
● Cooperation within the group and between groups		
● Attention given during other groups' presentations		
● Completed group evaluation		
Presentation		
● Organized logically		
● Concise		
● Text used appropriately		
● Images used appropriately		

COMMENTS

Grading Scale	
12–13 points = A	*8* points = D
11 points = B	*0–7* points = F
9–10 points = C	

Thank you to Cathy Glick (Hamilton Southeastern High School, Hamilton Southeastern Schools, Indiana) for providing the ideas for this checklist. (*Standards from Indiana Department of Education. [n.d.]. *Indiana academic standards.* Retrieved March 8, 2004, from http://www.indianastandards.org/)

■ HIGH SCHOOL CHECKLIST 2 ■

COURSE/CLASS _Chemistry_   **GRADE** _High School_

STANDARDS* _C.1.41: Describe the role of light, heat, and electrical energies in physical, chemical, and nuclear changes._
C.1.42: Describe that the energy release per gram of material is much larger in nuclear fusion or fission reactions than in chemical reactions. The change in mass (calculated by $E=mc^2$) is small but significant in nuclear reactions.
C.1.43: Calculate the amount of radioactive substance remaining after an integral number of half-lives have passed.

ACTIVITY _Perform a lab experiment on the effect of distance and shielding on radioactive particles._

CRITERIA/PERFORMANCE INDICATORS	Unprepared [0]	Ready for Anything [1]
Lab Group Dynamics		
● Participation by each member		
● Cooperation within the group		
● Cooperation between groups		
Lab Techniques		
● Pre-lab questions completed		
● Lab kept neat during experiment and cleaned up at conclusion of experiment		
● Proper care used in handling lab equipment		
● Safety rules followed		
Lab Analysis		
● Accurate graph depicts the relationship between distance and radiation amounts		
● Accurate graph illustrates the relationship between shielding and radiation amounts		
● Conclusions reflect evidence observed in the lab concerning the effect of distance and shielding on radioactive particles		
●		
●		
●		
●		

COMMENTS

Grading Scale
_10_ points = A   _7_ points = D
_9_ points = B   _0–6_ points = F
_8_ points = C

Thank you to Cathy Glick (Hamilton Southeastern High School, Hamilton Southeastern Schools, Indiana) for providing the ideas for this checklist. (*Standards from Indiana Department of Education. [n.d.]. _Indiana academic standards._ Retrieved March 8, 2004, from http://www.indianastandards.org/)

CHAPTER 4

Rubrics

WHAT ARE RUBRICS?

Rubrics are tools for assessing student products, projects, or performances. Rubrics measure students' mastery of content and thinking skills. Rubrics help students know what they need to do as well as understand the qualities their work must display. Rubrics allow teachers to assess and track numerical data in an expanded way (Schmoker, 1996). Every rubric includes these components:

- Rating scale

- Criteria that reflect standards

- Indicators for each level of performance

- Scoring system

- Grading scale

Figure 4.1 features a rubric template. (For a blank template you can use to create your own rubric, see the Examples section at the end of this chapter). The first row comprises the rating scale. The left column features the criteria and indictors. Columns two through five list evidence for each criterion and for each level of mastery. The sixth column gives delineates the score for each row. At the bottom of the rubric is a grading scale.

FIGURE 4.1 **Rubric Template**

▪ RUBRIC TEMPLATE ▪

COURSE/CLASS _____ GRADE _____

STANDARDS _____

ACTIVITY _____

SCORING / CRITERIA	1 Lowest Level	2 Emerging Level	3 Mastery Level	4 Exemplary Level	SCORE
FIRST CRITERION • Indicator • Indicator • Indicator	Evidence(s) for *first* criterion at *lowest* level of performance	Evidence(s) for *first* criterion at *second* level of performance	Evidence(s) for *first* criterion at *third* level of performance	Evidence(s) for *first* criterion at *highest* level of performance	__ x __ = ____ (total)
SECOND CRITERION • Indicator • Indicator • Indicator	Evidence(s) for *second* criterion at *lowest* level of performance	Evidence(s) for *second* criterion at *second* level of performance	Evidence(s) for *second* criterion at *third* level of performance	Evidence(s) for *second* criterion at *highest* level of performance	__ x __ = ____ (total)
THIRD CRITERION • Indicator • Indicator • Indicator	Evidence(s) for *third* criterion at *lowest* level of performance	Evidence(s) for *third* criterion at *second* level of performance	Evidence(s) for *third* criterion at *third* level of performance	Evidence(s) for *third* criterion at *highest* level of performance	__ x __ = ____ (total)
FOURTH CRITERION • Indicator • Indicator • Indicator	Evidence(s) for *fourth* criterion at *lowest* level of performance	Evidence(s) for *fourth* criterion at *second* level of performance	Evidence(s) for *fourth* criterion at *third* level of performance	Evidence(s) for *fourth* criterion at *highest* level of performance	__ x __ = ____ (total)
FIFTH CRITERION • Indicator • Indicator • Indicator	Evidence(s) for *fifth* criterion at *lowest* level of performance	Evidence(s) for *fifth* criterion at *second* level of performance	Evidence(s) for *fifth* criterion at *third* level of performance	Evidence(s) for *fifth* criterion at *highest* level of performance	__ x __ = ____ (total)
SIXTH CRITERION • Indicator • Indicator • Indicator	Evidence(s) for *sixth* criterion at *lowest* level of performance	Evidence(s) for *sixth* criterion at *second* level of performance	Evidence(s) for *sixth* criterion at *third* level of performance	Evidence(s) for *sixth* criterion at *highest* level of performance	__ x __ = ____ (total)

COMMENT:

____ = A
____ = B
____ = C
____ = D
____ = F

Final Score _____

Final Grade _____

HOW TO CREATE RUBRICS

Preplanning for Rubrics

Preplanning for rubrics is similar to preplanning for checklists. Just as it is with checklists, it is important to match the rubric to the standards and outcomes targeted for the project, product, or performance. If you spent time preplanning a checklist(s), review your preplanning and then follow the steps for creating a rubric described below. If you did not use a checklist(s), turn to Preplanning for Checklists. Follow the procedure described in chapter 3 before completing the steps for creating a rubric described below.

Steps for Creating Rubrics

Step 1: Create a Rating Scale

Most rubrics use a four-point scale. You may choose a scale from 1 to 4 or from 0 to 3. Whichever scale you choose, follow these guidelines:

- The first number on the rating scale should represent nonmastery or no work. You may choose to use 0 to represent the absence of work so as not to award a single point for no work. Or you may choose to use 1 to represent nonmastery of the work.

- The second number on the rating scale represents an attempt at the work, an emerging effort toward mastery, but not mastery. The second number on the scale represents an unsatisfactory rating.

- The third number on the scale represents mastery of content.

- The fourth number on the scale represents exemplary mastery.

Some teachers use a five-point scale to mimic traditional letter grades. However, teachers are encouraged to use a four-point scale instead because a four-point scale forces teachers to avoid assigning a middle-of-the-road rating (i.e., a C) and to decide whether or not students have achieved mastery. The middle rating is not helpful for students, because it indicates that they did not fail, they do not need remediation, and yet they have not achieved mastery. This neither encourages students to try harder nor does it guide them in how to improve their work.

Whichever rating scale you choose, be sure to create descriptive headings for the scale. These descriptors help students understand the ratings. (Remember, if you are teaching preschool or elementary students, you may create a pictorial scale. See chapter 3 for a further explanation of pictorial rating scales.) Figure 4.2 shows a rating scale that uses both descriptive headings and numbers.

| FIGURE 4.2 | Sample Rating Scale for a Rubric |

SCORING	1	2	3	4
	Not Yet	Student Council Elections	Senate Floor	Presidential Debates

From Burke, K. (1999). *The mindful school: How to assess authentic learning* (p. 88). Arlington Heights, IL: SkyLight Training and Publishing.

Step 2: Determine Criteria and Indicators

List the standards or critical learning to be evidenced in the assessment as criteria (broad categories) followed by indicators (specific categories). For an example, see Figure 4.3. "Organization" is the criterion and the bulleted items ("Hook," "Transitions," "Closure") are indicators. Be sure to include criteria and indicators for every standard you wish to assess.

| FIGURE 4.3 | Sample Criteria for a Rubric: Rubric for Assessing a Speech |

SCORING / CRITERIA	1	2	3	4	
	Not Yet	Student Council Elections	Senate Floor	Presidential Debates	Score
ORGANIZATION • Hook • Transitions • Closure					
CONTENT • Accuracy • Documentation • Quotations					
DELIVERY • Eye contact • Volume • Gestures					
VISUAL AID • Graphics • Appeal • Relevance					

Adapted from Burke, K. (1999). *The mindful school: How to assess authentic learning* (p. 88). Arlington Heights, IL: SkyLight Training and Publishing.

Step 3: Delineate Evidence(s) for Each Scoring Level

After you have carefully determined criteria and indicators, take time to delineate evidence(s) for each scoring level. The best approach is to begin with what an exemplary example might look like. For example, the delivery of an exemplary speech would include constant eye contact, steady and audible volume, and many appropriate gestures (see the Presidential Debates column in Figure 4.4). Write these evidences in the exemplary speech column. Be sure to delineate evidences for each criterion and indicator.

Second, imagine what an adequate, mastery level speech might look like. Write these evidences in the mastery level column (see the Senate Floor column in Figure 4.4). Be sure to delineate evidences for each criterion and indicator.

Third, imagine what an emerging attempt at a speech might look like. Write these evidences in the emerging level column (see the Student Council Elections column in Figure 4.4). Be sure to delineate evidences for each criterion and indicator.

Fourth, imagine what a nonmastery or no-work speech might look like. Write these evidences in the lowest level column (see the Not Yet column in Figure 4.4). Be sure to delineate evidences for each criterion and indicator.

Figure 4.4 on the following page shows criteria, indicators, and evidences for each level of performance of a speech.

The rubric is a picture of performance from the lowest to the highest form of achievement. Rubrics "measure degrees of quality" (Burke, 1999, p. 9). For project and performance assessments to be objective, teachers must use objective means to measure evidence of learning. The rubric provides an objective and valid means to assess learning.

Step 4: Create Scoring and Grading Scales

The final step is to create scoring and grading scales. You might choose to score each criterion the same, giving the same weight to each standard. Or you might choose to score each criterion differently, giving more weight to one standard over another. For example, you might decide to give speech content more weight than speech delivery. See Figure 4.5 on page 51 for an example of a weighted scoring scale.

After you have determined your scoring scale, create a traditional grading scale to match it. This will allow you to assign a letter grade to the rubric so that students and parents understand how well students performed on the project, product, or performance.

FIGURE 4.4	Sample Evidences for a Rubric

■ RUBRIC FOR ASSESSING A SPEECH ■

COURSE/CLASS _Language Arts_ GRADE __8__

STANDARD _Speak effectively using language appropriate to the situation and audience._

ACTIVITY _Students will present a five-minute persuasive speech._

SCORING / CRITERIA	1 Not Yet	2 Student Council Elections	3 Senate Floor	4 Presidential Debates	SCORE
ORGANIZATION • Hook • Transitions • Closure	• None • None • None	• Introduces topic • Uses words to link ideas • Lacks interest	• Grabs attention • Makes key connections between ideas • Refers to closure in introduction	• Electrifies audience • Smooth flow of ideas • Powerful and dramatic	_ x _ = ____ (total)
CONTENT • Accuracy • Documentation • Quotations	• 3 or more factual errors • No sources cited • No quotes	• 2 factual errors • 1 source cited • 1 quote to support case	• 1 factual error • 2 sources cited • 2 quotes to support case	• All information is correct • 3 or more sources cited • 3 key quotes to prove case	_ x _ = ____ (total)
DELIVERY • Eye contact • Volume • Gestures	• Reads speech • Cannot be heard • None	• Looks at some people some of the time • Can be heard by people in front • Uses a few gestures	• Looks at some people all of the time • Can be heard by most people • Uses some gestures appropriately	• Looks at all the people all of the time • Can be heard clearly by most people • Uses many appropriate, effective gestures	_ x _ = ____ (total)
VISUAL AID • Graphics • Appeal • Relevance	• None • None • None	• Minimal • Little visual appeal • Minimal relation-ship to topic	• Colorful • Captures audi-ence's attention • Relates specifically to topic	• Creative graphics that enhance speech • Visually stimulates audience • Relates and reinforces topic	_ x _ = ____ (total)

COMMENTS:

18–20	=	A
15–17	=	B
10–14	=	C
<9	=	Not Yet

Final Score _____

Final Grade _____

Adapted from Burke, K. (1999). _The mindful school: How to assess authentic learning_ (p. 88). Arlington Heights, IL: SkyLight Training and Publishing.

FIGURE 4.5   **Sample Weighted Scoring Scale for a Rubric**

■ RUBRIC FOR ASSESSING A SPEECH ■

COURSE/CLASS ___*Language Arts*___   GRADE ___*8*___
STANDARD *Speak effectively using language appropriate to the situation and audience.*
ACTIVITY ___*Students will present a five-minute persuasive speech.*___

SCORING / CRITERIA	1 Not Yet	2 Student Council Elections	3 Senate Floor	4 Presidential Debates	SCORE
ORGANIZATION • Hook • Transitions • Closure	• None • None • None	• Introduces topic • Uses words to link ideas • Lacks interest	• Grabs attention • Makes key connections between ideas • Refers to closure in introduction	• Electrifies audience • Smooth flow of ideas • Powerful and dramatic	___ x 5 = ___ (total)
CONTENT • Accuracy • Documentation • Quotations	• 3 or more factual errors • No sources cited • No quotes	• 2 factual errors • 1 source cited • 1 quote to support case	• 1 factual error • 2 sources cited • 2 quotes to support case	• All information is correct • 3 or more sources cited • 3 key quotes to prove case	___ x 10 = ___ (total)
DELIVERY • Eye contact • Volume • Gestures	• Reads speech • Cannot be heard • None	• Looks at some people some of the time • Can be heard by people in front • Uses a few gestures	• Looks at some people all of the time • Can be heard by most people • Uses some gestures appropriately	• Looks at all the people all of the time • Can be heard clearly by most people • Uses many appropriate, effective gestures	___ x 5 = ___ (total)
VISUAL AID • Graphics • Appeal • Relevance	• None • None • None	• Minimal • Little visual appeal • Minimal relationship to topic	• Colorful • Captures our attention • Relates specifically to topic	• Creative graphics that enhance speech • Visually stimulates audience • Relates and reinforces topic	___ x 10 = ___ (total)

COMMENTS:

81–90	=	A
72–80	=	B
63–71	=	C
54–62	=	D
0–53	=	F

Final Score   ___/(90)

Final Grade   ___

Adapted from Burke, K. (1999). *The mindful school: How to assess authentic learning* (p. 88). Arlington Heights, IL: SkyLight Training and Publishing.

Why Bother with Rubrics?

With all the time constraints placed upon teachers today, developing a rubric might seem like just another item on a teacher's to-do list. However, rubrics often save teachers time in the end, as well as lead to more effective assessment methods for teachers and students. Following are the top ten reasons why rubrics are well worth the effort.

10 With all the demands on teachers today, these easy, reliable assessment tools improve the efficiency of teaching.

9 Rubrics make grading faster, not slower. Think about this brief scenario a moment: You must assign a grade to a student's science project (e.g., a demonstration of the inside of a volcano). You remember the instructions you gave at the beginning of the project, and now you are faced with an outcome. If you do not use a rubric, you may fall into the trap of deciding whether or not you like the project and assigning a grade based on this subjective assessment project. However, if you use a rubric, you can assess the project using concrete guidelines and easily formulate an overall grade.

8 Rubrics tend to be more objective and fair than single letter grades, because the criteria are set and communicated to students prior to the start of the project. Students know what you expect and they strive for mastery. If students hit the target, they receive a good grade. Students know that grading is fair and consistent.

7 Rubrics communicate to parents exactly what is expected of students. Parents no longer view grades as a mystery. They recognize that you are competent, well prepared, and fair in your judgments.

6 Rubrics are time-efficient, because goals are set at the outset of the unit immediately after learning goals are established. Remember, the shortest distance between two points is a straight line. Knowing where you're going helps you to navigate a straight course. Time is saved when you match instruction and assessment from the very start of the unit.

5 Rubrics provide students with feedback about their performance. Rather than seeing a letter grade and a few teacher comments on the page, students receive feedback for each criterion and indicator.

4 Rubrics can be created with student input. Once the teacher establishes the standards, concepts, skills, and processes for the unit, the teacher can invite students to help create the rubric. This process helps students "buy in" to the rubric from the outset. For directions on how to create rubrics with student input, see Figure 4.6.

3 Rubrics can be used as a teacher-student conferencing tool designed to improve student performance, affirm a job well done, or design corrective measures encouraging mastery level work. The teacher can use the rubric to conduct student conferences and set goals for the next learning step.

2 Rubrics help teachers remain focused on the process of learning as the curriculum develops. When the teacher lays out criteria prior to instruction, he or she is more likely to maintain focus on the criteria throughout instruction. When students know the criteria from the outset, they tend to be more focused in their learning as well. Teachers can act as facilitators, mentors, and guides when students understand where they are going and what they are striving for.

1 Finally, rubrics tell a story while isolated grades only provide a title.

FIGURE 4.6   Creating Rubrics with Student Input

1.   Before you create a rubric with students, be sure you know exactly what standards you wish to assess. Spend time preplanning just as you would if you were creating the rubric on your own.

2.   Draw a template on the chalkboard, overhead projector, or chart paper. Write the rating scale (numbers only) in the top row. The template should look like this:

Score / Criteria	1	2	3	4	

3.   Write the criteria and indicators in the first column. Explain to students that these criteria are nonnegotiable because they represent the standards students must meet to pass the class.

4.   Ask students to help you develop measurable evidence for each criterion and indicator at each level. Encourage students to imagine what an exemplary performance might look like. They may think to themselves, "I'll do this for a 3 and that for a 4!" Use one of the following methods to direct students in delineating evidences:

FIGURE 4.6   **Creating Rubrics with Student Input (continued)**

a. Assign each cooperative group to select a specific criterion with indicators and create evidence for each level of performance. When each group has completed its task, encourage the whole class to review the evidences and reach consensus on what evidences should be included on the final rubric.

b. Work together as a whole class. Determine evidence for every level of performance to match criteria and indicators.

c. Before students contribute ideas, give students examples by filling in a random cell for each criterion. Then encourage students to work as a class or in groups to complete the rubric.

5. Add the scoring and grading scale. If you use weighted scores, explain why some criteria receive more weight than others.

6. Review the rubric with students. Initiate a class discussion to answer students' questions and clarify wording. Make sure that the rubric clearly defines the project and is challenging, yet attainable.

Note: Before students create a "real" rubric, you might choose to help them understand the rubric-building process by leading them to create a "fun" rubric. Constructing a fun rubric motivates students to embrace the rubric-building process. Following is a sample fun rubric for assessing a movie:

SCORING / CRITERIA	1 No Way!	2 I Don't Think So!	3 I'm There!	4 Absolutely! This Rules!
THE MOVIE	A foreign film and I don't understand the language. I thought it was something different.	A matinee full of little kids screaming and throwing popcorn. Plus the movie was dull and boring.	Adventure, thrills, and a lot of stars my age that were so cool.	This one had me on the edge of my seat—time flew! Gotta see it again. I'm buying the video!
THE FOOD	Fruit from home.	Gum.	Biggie popcorn with a biggie cola.	Free food, all you can eat!
THE COMPANY	I went alone and sat by someone talking on a cell phone.	I went with a family member, but nobody saw me!	I went with a group of really good friends.	I had the dream date of a lifetime and we held hands!
AFTER THE MOVIE	Dad picked me up with a minivan full of his bowling buddies.	We left and went home.	We went out for pizza and met more friends. We had a blast!	We went for a sandwich, talked for 2 hours, and set up another date.

— ■ —

Rubrics provide authentic assessment at a glance. They show evidence of learning from the whole unit and accurately reflect the quality of student learning. Rubrics can be included in student portfolios and can be compared with other rubrics to demonstrate student growth and achievement over time.

Examples

Following are several rubrics: a rubric template and sample rubrics for elementary, middle, and high school levels. These rubrics correspond to the sample performance tasks and checklists for the equivalent grade levels provided in chapters 2 and 3. (See the appendices for additional sample rubrics.)

▪ RUBRIC TEMPLATE ▪

COURSE/CLASS _____ GRADE _____

STANDARDS_____

ACTIVITY _____

SCORING / CRITERIA	1 Lowest Level	2 Emerging Level	3 Mastery Level	4 Exemplary Level	SCORE
					__ x __ = ____
					__ x __ = ____
					__ x __ = ____
					__ x __ = ____
					__ x __ = ____
					__ x __ = ____

COMMENT:

____ = A
____ = B
____ = C
____ = D
____ = F

Final Score ____

Final Grade ____

■ ELEMENTARY RUBRIC ■

COURSE/CLASS _Writing and math_   **GRADE** _Kindergarten_

STANDARDS _Mathematics. Geometry standard: Students identify common objects around them and describe their geometric features and position. Language arts. Standard 5 for writing process: Students begin to write and draw pictures for specific purposes and specific audiences._

ACTIVITY _Each student creates an eight-page book; each page of the book features one of the eight shapes—circle, square, oval, rectangle, diamond, heart, triangle, or star. Students use magazine clippings, digital or conventional pictures, and drawings of shapes found in the environment._

SCORING / CRITERIA	1 Not Yet	2 Emerging Level	3 Mastery Level	4 Exemplary Level	SCORE
PICTURES OF EACH SHAPE	Student uses random pictures that do not depict the correct shapes.	Student uses at least one shape picture on four pages of the book.	Student uses at least one shape picture on all eight pages of the book.	Student uses several shape pictures on all eight pages of the book.	_ x 1 = ____

COMMENTS

4	=	A
3	=	B
2	=	C
1	=	D
0	=	F

Final Score ____/(4)

Final Grade ____

Thank you to Jenni LaMar (Lebanon Middle School, Lebanon Community Schools, Indiana) and Linda Snyder (Center Grove Community Schools, Indiana) for providing the ideas for this checklist.

▪ MIDDLE SCHOOL RUBRIC ▪

COURSE/CLASS ___Social Studies___ GRADE _6_

STANDARDS* 6.3.1: *Explain the components of most maps (title, scale, legend, grid, and projection). Compare different map types (topographic, thematic, etc.) and different map projections, and explain the appropriate use for each. 6.3.3: Identify the names and locations of countries and major cities in Europe and the Western Hemisphere. Identify the states of Mexico and the provinces of Canada. 6.3.4: Describe major physical characteristics (natural features, such as land and water forms, climate, natural vegetation, and native wildlife) of regions in Europe and the Americas. 6.3.5: Describe major cultural characteristics (human features, such as population characteristics, communication and transportation networks, religion and customs, and how people make a living or build homes and other structures) of regions in Europe and the Western Hemisphere. 6.3.10: Compare and contrast cultural patterns—such as language, religion, and ethnicity—in various parts of Europe; the Caribbean; and North, South, and Central America. 6.5.7: Examine art, music, literature, and architecture in Europe and the Americas; explain their relationship to the societies that created them; and give examples of how artistic ideas have spread from one culture to another. 6.5.8: Use a variety of resources, including newspapers, magazines, Web sites, and databases, to collect and analyze data on cultural factors in countries of Europe and the Americas. Use charts, graphs, and other data to compare and hypothesize the relation of these factors to a nation's development.*

ACTIVITY ___Conduct research about your assigned region of Latin America. Make a proposal for visiting this region on spring break. Your trip should include popular tourist sites, historical landmarks, culture of the area, interesting or unique landforms, and a map of your travel route.___

SCORING / CRITERIA	1 Tour Group Is Wandering Throughout Latin America	2 Made It to the Airport, But Missed the Plane	3 On the Next Trip You Could Be the Guide	4 You Could Publish Your Own Travel Guide	SCORE
ACCURACY OF INFORMATION	Picked up the wrong map for your trip (3 or more mistakes).	You had a road-block and a bridge out in your information (2 mistakes).	You had only one roadblock in your information (1 mistake).	All items are accurate and well researched.	___ x 5 = ___ (20)
GROUP PRESENTATION • Everyone participates • Eye contact	Lost some group members along the way. (Only one group member did the presentation.)	Most of your members stayed with you through-out your trip. (Two group members did the presentation.)	The group stayed together until one member got sidetracked. (Three group members did the presentation.)	The entire group started and ended the tour together. (Everyone did the presentation.)	___ x 5 = ___ (20)
CONTENT • Tourist sites • Historical landmarks • Culture of the area • Landforms • Map of travel route	When you returned to tell your family about your trip, they couldn't fig-ure out where you'd been.	Your friends and family are only slightly interested in possibly booking a trip to your desti-nation due to the few details you remembered about your trip.	Your friends and family are ready to board the next plane due to your recap of your trip.	Your friends and family are ready to support you in opening your own travel business due to your excellent knowledge of Latin America.	___ x 5 = ___ (20)
CREATIVITY • Colorful • Many pictures • Neat • Organized	You forgot the color film for the camera.	You only bought 200-speed film for the camera, so some of the pic-tures didn't turn out.	You were well prepared and had the right film so that all of your pictures turned out.	You could be hired by National Geographic as an on-site photographer.	___ x 5 = ___ (20)

COMMENTS		
	72–80 = A	
	64–71 = B	Final Score _____/(80)
	56–63 = C	
	48–55 = D	Final Grade _____
	0–47 = F	

*(Standards from Indiana Department of Education. [n.d.] *Indiana academic standards.* Retrieved March 8, 2004, from http://indianastandards.org/)

▪ HIGH SCHOOL RUBRIC ▪

COURSE/CLASS _Chemistry_   **GRADE** _High School_

STANDARDS* _C.1.43: Calculate the amount of radioactive substance remaining after an integral number of half-lives have passed._

ACTIVITY _Complete a lab experiment to determine the half-life of radioactive isotopes._

SCORING CRITERIA	1 Nuclear Meltdown	2 Heisenberg's Uncertainty	3 Manhattan Project	4 As Bright as the Sun	SCORE
TITLE, PURPOSE, AND BACKGROUND	Title is not related to lab, purpose is unclear, and background information is not given.	Title is related to lab, purpose is clear, but background information is unrelated to lab.	Title is related to lab, purpose is clear, and background information shows some research.	Title reflects nature of lab. Purpose and background information show understanding and insight.	___ x 5 = ___ (20)
MATERIALS AND PROCEDURE	Key materials are not listed, and key steps are missing.	Most materials are listed, but procedural steps are unclear.	All materials are listed, and step-by-step procedures are included.	All materials are listed, and step-by-step procedures could be followed by someone else.	___ x 5 = ___ (20)
DATA	Data is written haphazardly.	Data is placed in table format.	Data is placed in table format with variables indicated.	Data is placed in table format with title and variables indicated.	___ x 5 = ___ (20)
GRAPH	Data points are shown on correct axes.	Data points are shown correctly with labeled axes.	Data points are shown correctly with labeled axes and a title at the top.	Data points are shown correctly with labeled axes, a title at the top, and a best fit line or curve.	___ x 5 = ___ (20)
ANALYSIS OF DATA	Graph was used to calculate half-life.	Graph was used to calculate half-life, and percent error was also calculated.	Graph was used to calculate half-life and percent error. Sources of error are realistic.	The sources of error are realistic and do not include measurements or calculations.	___ x 5 = ___ (20)

COMMENTS:

91–100	=	A
81–90	=	B
71–80	=	C
61–70	=	D
0–60	=	F

Final Score   _____/(100)_

Final Grade   _____

Thank you to Cathy Glick (Hamilton Southeastern High School, Hamilton Southeastern Schools, Indiana) for providing the ideas for this rubric. (*Standard from Indiana Department of Education. [n.d.]. _Indiana academic standards._ Retrieved March 8, 2004, from http://www.indianastandards.org/)

▪ HIGH SCHOOL RUBRIC 2 ▪

COURSE/CLASS _Chemistry_ **GRADE** _High School_

STANDARDS* C.1.41: Describe the role of light, heat, and electrical energies in physical, chemical, and nuclear changes.
C.1.42: Describe that the energy release per gram of material is much larger in nuclear fusion or fission reactions than in chemical reactions. The change in mass (calculated by $E=mc^2$) is small but significant in nuclear reactions.
C.1.43: Calculate the amount of radioactive substance remaining after an integral number of half-lives have passed.

ACTIVITY _Write a report to the power company. Include the following information that you learned from the group presentations: how a nuclear power plant works, how to dispose of nuclear waste, potential health risks, proposed site for the plant and population data within a 5-, 10-, 15-, 20-, and 25-mile radius, and alternative energy sources._

SCORING / CRITERIA	1 Below Standards	2 Almost Meets Standards	3 Meets Standards	4 Exceeds Standards	SCORE
WRITING PROCESS • Report has introduction, supporting paragraphs, and a conclusion. • Proper grammar and spelling are used.	• Report is unclear and difficult to understand. • More than 15 mistakes made.	• All elements are present, but with little evidence to support conclusion. • 10–15 mistakes made.	• All elements are present; some evidence is given to support conclusion. • 5–10 mistakes made.	• All elements are present; the evidence given to support conclusion is meaningful. • Fewer than 5 mistakes made.	__ x 5 = __ (20) __ x 5 = __ (20)
UNDERSTANDING OF NUCLEAR ENERGY • Half-life of radioactive isotope • Fission reactions • Effect of shielding and distance on radioactive particles	• Half-life is mentioned, but without an attempt to determine decay rates of nuclear waste. • Nuclear fission is identified as the type of reaction used in a nuclear power plant. • Shielding and distance are mentioned, but the effect is not indicated.	• An estimate of the decay rate of nuclear waste is given. • Uranium is highlighted as the fuel source in a nuclear power plant. • Shielding and distance are used to discuss the location of where the plant should be built.	• Calculations for the decay of nuclear waste are made but are inaccurate. • Fission is mentioned as part of the explanation of how a nuclear power plant works. • Shielding and distance are used to discuss the location of where the plant should be built with evidence from labs cited.	• Calculations for the decay of nuclear waste are accurate. • Detailed information about nuclear fission and nuclear power is given. • Shielding and distance are used to discuss the location of where and how the plant should be built with evidence from labs cited and explained.	__ x 5 = __ (20) __ x 5 = __ (20) __ x 5 = __ (20)
INCORPORATION OF INFORMATION FROM GROUP PRESENTATIONS • Health risks • Alternatives to nuclear energy • How a nuclear plant works • Sites on which to build a plant • Methods of nuclear waste disposal	• Health risks are mentioned. • Alternatives are mentioned. • How the plant works is mentioned. • Sites are mentioned. • Nuclear waste disposal is mentioned.	• Information about health risks is present, but it shows little evidence of understanding. • Information about alternatives is present, but it shows little evidence of understanding. • Information about how a nuclear power plant works is present, but it shows little evidence of understanding. • Information about sites is present, but it shows little evidence of understanding. • Information about nuclear waste disposal is present, but it shows little evidence of understanding.	• Understanding about health risks is evident, but details are missing. • Understanding about alternatives is evident, but details are missing. • Understanding about how a nuclear power plant works is evident, but details are missing. • Understanding about sites is evident, but details are missing. • Understanding about nuclear waste disposal is evident, but details are missing.	• Detailed, coherent information about health risks is given. • Detailed, coherent information about alternatives given. • Detailed, coherent information about how a nuclear power plant works is given. • Detailed, coherent information about sites is given. • Detailed, coherent information about nuclear waste disposal is given.	__ x 5 = __ (20) __ x 5 = __ (20) __ x 5 = __ (20) __ x 5 = __ (20) __ x 5 = __ (20)

COMMENTS:

185–200	= A
170–184	= B
148–169	= C
130–147	= D
0–129	= F

Final Score _____/(200)

Final Grade _____

Thank you to Cathy Glick (Hamilton Southeastern High School, Hamilton Southeastern Schools, Indiana) for providing the ideas for this rubric. (*Standard from Indiana Department of Education. [n.d.]. _Indiana academic standards._ Retrieved March 8, 2004, from http://www.indianastandards.org/)

CHAPTER 5

Putting It All Together

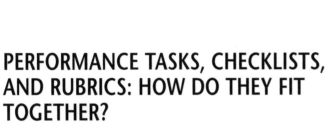

PERFORMANCE TASKS, CHECKLISTS, AND RUBRICS: HOW DO THEY FIT TOGETHER?

As discussed in chapter 1, assessments are communication tools that are a critical part of the student-teacher relationship. When used well, they allow teachers to better define their goals and students to better understand what they need to know and be able to do to achieve success.

Performance tasks, checklists, and rubrics are assessment tools that can help to clarify expectations for both teachers and students. We've learned about these tools and viewed examples of each in the previous chapters. Each tool is valuable when used on its own, but even more valuable when used together with the other tools. Each tool builds upon the other.

Let's examine how this progression works by looking at a performance task. As the teacher develops a performance task, he or she essentially creates the assessments that will measure students' learning within the task. Figure 5.1 shows an example of a performance task that a teacher created to assess a science project on circuits and energy usage.

FIGURE 5.1   Sample Performance Task

■ PERFORMANCE TASK FOR EIGHTH GRADE SCIENCE ■

COURSE/CLASS _Science_   GRADE   _8_

STANDARDS* *8.3.19: Investigate and compare series and parallel circuits.*
8.3.20: Compare the differences in power consumption in different electrical devices.

TASK DESCRIPTION

Indianapolis Power and Light in conjunction with the Environmental Protection Agency is investigating the current public understanding of circuitry and power consumption in the Midwest. All eighth-grade science classes will investigate the differences between series and parallel circuits and compare the power consumption of different appliances. Students will present their results on April 30.

DIRECT INSTRUCTION FOR WHOLE CLASS   The whole class will be involved in the following learning experience:

1. *Learn terminology: series circuits, parallel circuits, and kilowatt-hours.*
2. *Review group dynamics (task assignments for each member) and social skills (politeness and cooperation).*
3. *Discuss safety procedures.*
4. *Review PowerPoint basics.*

GROUP WORK

Group One	Group Two	Group Three	Group Four	Group Five
Conduct research about series circuits and build a series circuit board.	*Conduct research about parallel circuits and build a parallel circuit board.*	*Investigate how much power different appliances use. Create a poster that features appliances and the energy they use.*	*Create a PowerPoint presentation comparing and contrasting series and parallel circuits.*	*Create a PowerPoint presentation comparing energy usage of older appliances (more than 10 years old) and newer appliances.*

INDIVIDUAL WORK

1. *Create a poster highlighting what you have learned from the group presentations.*
2. *Make a graph that compares the energy usage of five appliances.*
3. *Write a journal reflection about why using energy-efficient appliances is important for future energy conservation.*

METHODS OF ASSESSMENT

1. *Checklist to assess each group's project*
2. *Rubric to assess individual projects*
3. *Teacher-made test on series and parallel circuits*

Thank you to Donna Harper (Lincoln Middle School, MSD of Pike Township, Indiana) for providing the ideas for this performance task. (*Standards from Indiana Department of Education. [n.d.]. *Indiana academic standards.* Retrieved March 10, 2004, from http://www.indianastandards.org/)

Once the teacher has developed a performance task, he or she can use it as a jumping-off point to develop a checklist. The checklist features what the teacher wants students to know and be able to do related to the project or content. The teacher can use the task description, group work, and individual work from the performance task to define the criteria in the checklist. For example, the teacher might create a checklist for each of the group projects listed in the performance task (see Figure 5.1). First, the teacher would list the group task, and then the teacher would develop specific criteria for completing the task. These criteria would be included on the checklist. Student groups can use the checklist to discern whether or not they are on the right track. The checklist in Figure 5.2 demonstrates how the performance task featured in Figure 5.1 lends itself to checklist development.

FIGURE 5.2 **Sample Checklist**

▪ CHECKLIST FOR EIGHTH GRADE SCIENCE ▪

COURSE/CLASS _Science_   **GRADE** _8_

STANDARDS* _8.3.19: Investigate and compare series and parallel circuits._
8.3.20: Compare the differences in power consumption in different electrical devices.

ACTIVITY _**Group 1** builds a series circuit board. **Group 2** builds a parallel circuit board. **Group 3** creates a poster that features appliances and the energy they use. **Group 4** creates a PowerPoint presentation comparing series and parallel circuits. **Group 5** creates a PowerPoint presentation comparing energy usage of older and newer appliances._

CRITERIA/PERFORMANCE INDICATORS	Not Yet [0]	Yes [1]
Group 1: Series Circuit Board		
• Used 3 lights and 1 switch.		
• Wiring is completed.		
• When switch is closed, all lights are on.		
• When any light is removed, all lights are extinguished.		
Group 2: Parallel Circuit Board		
• Used 3 lights and 1 switch.		
• Wiring is completed.		
• When switch is closed, all lights are on.		
• When any light is removed, remaining lights stay lit.		
Group 3: Poster of Appliances and Energy Usage		
• Used 5 appliances.		
• Chart of energy usage is completed.		
• Used color.		
• Poster is neat and completed.		

COMMENTS

Scale

4	=	A
3	=	B
2	=	C
1	=	D
0	=	F

Group 1

___	=	A
___	=	B
___	=	C
___	=	D
___	=	F

Group 2

___	=	A
___	=	B
___	=	C
___	=	D
___	=	F

Group 3

___	=	A
___	=	B
___	=	C
___	=	D
___	=	F

Thank you to Donna Harper (Lincoln Middle School, MSD of Pike Township, Indiana) for providing the ideas for this performance task. (*Standards from Indiana Department of Education. [n.d.]. _Indiana academic standards._ Retrieved March 10, 2004, from http://www.indianastandards.org/)

FIGURE 5.2 **Sample Checklist (continued)**

■ CHECKLIST FOR EIGHTH GRADE SCIENCE ■

COURSE/CLASS *Science*   GRADE   *8*

STANDARDS* *8.3.19: Investigate and compare series and parallel circuits.*
8.3.20: Compare the differences in power consumption in different electrical devices.

ACTIVITY   **Group 1** *builds a series circuit board.* **Group 2** *builds a parallel circuit board.* **Group 3** *creates a poster that features appliances and the energy they use.* **Group 4** *creates a PowerPoint presentation comparing series and parallel circuits.* **Group 5** *creates a PowerPoint presentation comparing energy usage of older and newer appliances.*

CRITERIA/PERFORMANCE INDICATORS	Not Yet [0]	Yes [1]
Group 4: PowerPoint Presentation Comparing Series and Parallel Circuits		
● *Text is clear and readable.*		
● *Information is accurate.*		
● *Transitions are smooth.*		
● *Sources are cited.*		
Group 5: PowerPoint Presentation Comparing Energy Usage of Older and Newer Appliances		
● *Text is clear and readable.*		
● *Information is accurate.*		
● *Transitions are smooth.*		
● *Sources are cited.*		

COMMENTS

Group 4

_____	=	A
_____	=	B
_____	=	C
_____	=	D
_____	=	F

Group 5

_____	=	A
_____	=	B
_____	=	C
_____	=	D
_____	=	F

Thank you to Donna Harper (Lincoln Middle School, MSD of Pike Township, Indiana) for providing the ideas for this performance task. (*Standards from Indiana Department of Education. [n.d.]. *Indiana academic standards.* Retrieved March 10, 2004, from http://www.indianastandards.org/)

Once the teacher has developed a checklist, he or she can follow a few simple steps to create a rubric. The checklist serves as a reminder of the key learning the teacher wants students to achieve from the content or project. The teacher begins by choosing a rating scale, and then expands the criteria from the checklist or creates new criteria to develop the rubric. Figure 5.3 shows the rubric a teacher developed to assess students' individual work: a poster highlighting what they learned, a graph comparing energy usage of five appliances, and a journal reflection about energy conservation.

— ■ —

When teachers create and coordinate performance tasks, checklists, and rubrics, they focus their teaching and save time. Students benefit by knowing what is expected of them at the beginning of the unit (via explanation of the performance task), during the unit (via use of checklists), and at the end of the unit (via assessment using a rubric).

FIGURE 5.3   **Sample Rubric**

■ RUBRIC FOR EIGHTH GRADE SCIENCE ■

COURSE/CLASS _Science_   GRADE _8_

STANDARDS* _8.3.19: Investigate and compare series and parallel circuits._
8.3.20: Compare the differences in power consumption in different electrical devices.

ACTIVITY _Students complete individual projects: (1) create a poster highlighting what they learned from the group presenta-_
tions; (2) make a graph that compares the energy usage of five appliances; (3) write a journal reflection about why using
energy-efficient appliances is important for future energy conservation.

SCORING CRITERIA	1 Not Yet	2 Almost	3 Meets Standards	4 Exceeds Standards	SCORE
POSTER • Includes information about series and parallel circuits. • Features information about energy usage of appliances.	• No information listed • No information included	• Inaccurate or incomplete data • Inaccurate or incomplete data	• Information correct; color used • Information correct; color used	• Information correct; very colorful graphics or pictures used • Information correct; very colorful graphics or pictures used	___ x 5 = ___ (20) ___ x 5 = ___ (20)
GRAPH • Uses 5 appliances. • Data is accurate. • Line graph is included.	• Fewer than 3 appliances compared • No data • No graph	• 3–4 appliances compared • Inaccurate or incomplete data • Wrong type of graph	• 5 appliances compared • Accurate data • Correct graph	• More than 5 appliances compared • Accurate data; energy labels displayed • Graph is visually appealing	___ x 5 = ___ (20) ___ x 5 = ___ (20) ___ x 5 = ___ (20)
JOURNAL ENTRY • Shows evidence of reason. • Presents supporting statistics. • Is one page long.	• Unclear reasoning and no conclusion • No supporting data • ⅓ page	• Some reasoning evident, but wrong conclusion • Inaccurate or incomplete data • ⅓ to ⅔ long	• Clear reasoning and conclusion • Accurate data • 1 page long	• Insightful reasoning with supportive data • Accurate data with sources stated • More than 1 page long	___ x 5 = ___ (20) ___ x 5 = ___ (20) ___ x 5 = ___ (20)

COMMENTS:

144–160 =	A
128–143 =	B
112–127 =	C
96–111 =	D
0–95 =	F

Final Score _____/(160)

Final Grade _____

Thank you to Donna Harper (Lincoln Middle School, MSD of Pike Township, Indiana) for providing the ideas for this performance task. (*Standards from Indiana Department of Education. [n.d.]. _Indiana academic standards._ Retrieved March 10, 2004, from http://www.indianastandards.org/)

Sample Assessment Sets

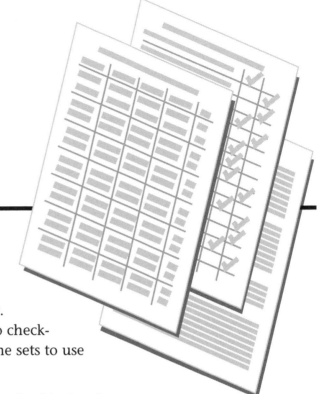

Appendix A features five sample assessment sets. Each set includes a performance task, one or two checklists, and a rubric. Adapt or borrow ideas from the sets to use in your classroom.

Many thanks to the teachers from the Teacher Leadership Academy who developed these assessment sets. (The Teacher Leadership Academy is sponsored by the Central Indiana Educational Service Center, 6321 LaPas Trail, Indianapolis, Indiana, 46268, 317-387-7100, http://www.ciesc.k12.in.us/.)

Example

American Revolution

❏ Performance Task

❏ Checklist

❏ Rubric

■ AMERICAN REVOLUTION PERFORMANCE TASK ■

COURSE/CLASS   _Social Studies_   GRADE   _5_

STANDARDS*

Social Studies

5.1.11: Analyze the causes of the Revolution, such as colonial resistance to British imperial policies, the denial of traditional rights of Englishmen to American colonists, and taxation without representation.

5.1.12: Identify major British and American leaders and describe their roles in key events, such as the First and Second Continental Congresses, drafting and approval of the Declaration of Independence (1776), publication of Common Sense, and major battles of the Revolutionary War.

5.1.13: Assess the influence of other countries, such as France, Spain, Russia, Germany, Poland, and the Netherlands, in the American Revolution; identify individuals from other countries who assisted the American cause.

5.1.14: Identify and evaluate contributions of women during the American Revolution, including Abigail Adams, Martha Washington, Mercy Otis Warren, and Molly Pitcher.

5.1.15: Explain consequences of the Revolution, including the drafting of state constitutions and the achievement of independence by the United States.

5.1.20: Read historical fiction and nonfiction about an event of the American Revolution and reconstruct the literal meaning of passages by identifying who was involved, what happened, where it happened, what events led to these developments, and what consequences or outcomes followed.

Language Arts

5.5.2: Write responses to literature that demonstrate an understanding of a literary work, support judgments through references to the text and to prior knowledge, and develop interpretations that exhibit careful reading and understanding.

5.5.3: Write research reports about important ideas, issues, or events by using the following guidelines: frame questions that direct the investigation; establish a main idea or topic; develop the topic with simple facts, details, examples, and explanations; and use a variety of information sources, including firsthand interviews, reference materials, and electronic resources, to locate information for the report.

5.5.4: Write persuasive letters or compositions that state a clear position in support of a proposal; support a position with relevant evidence and effective emotional appeals; follow a simple organizational pattern, with the most appealing statements first and the least powerful ones last; and address reader concerns.

5.5.5: Use note-taking skills.

5.6.3: Identify and correctly use appropriate tense for verbs that are often misused.

5.6.5: Use a colon to separate hours and minutes and to introduce a list; use quotation marks around the exact words of a speaker and titles of articles, poems, songs, short stories, and chapters in books; use semicolons and commas for transitions.

5.6.6: Use correct capitalization.

5.6.7: Spell roots or bases of words, prefixes, suffixes, contractions, and syllable constructions correctly.

TASK DESCRIPTION

As fifth-grade experts on American history, you have been asked to describe the American Revolution to the third- and fourth-graders. In this description, you will explain the consequences of the war in the United States. Some will write a newspaper editorial decrying taxation, others will create biographical reports about men and women involved in the Revolution, some will reenact a town meeting about colonial rights, others will create a scale model of battlefields, and some will imagine interviewing people from other countries who assisted during the Revolution. You will present your lesson at the third- and fourth-grade history fair.

(continued on next page)

Thank you to Jennie Buck (Wheeler Elementary, Speedway Schools, Indiana) for providing the ideas for this performance task. (*Standards adapted from Indiana Department of Education. [n.d.]. Indiana academic standards. Retrieved March 10, 2004, from http://www.indianastandards.org/)

▪ AMERICAN REVOLUTION PERFORMANCE TASK ▪

DIRECT INSTRUCTION FOR WHOLE CLASS | The whole class will be involved in the following learning experience:

1. Listen to a lecture and presentation of the facts of the Revolution (people and places).
2. Discuss important people and places.
3. Consult maps and trace routes of Revolutionary battles.
4. Listen to fiction and nonfiction readings about the Revolution.
5. Visit the library to conduct research.
6. Read textbook selections and articles (from the encyclopedia or Internet) about the Revolution.

GROUP WORK

Group One	Group Two	Group Three	Group Four	Group Five
Write a newspaper editorial persuading colonists to decry taxation. Be sure to explain how and why Britain taxed the colonies.	Create biographical presentations about men and women who contributed to the Revolution.	Reenact a town meeting in which key leaders discuss the denial of rights by the king and the consequences and alternatives for the colonists.	Design scale models of key battlefields. Include key historical players and depict important victories.	Imagine interviewing individuals from other countries who assisted in the American Revolution. Write about their background, what they might have said, why they participated in the Revolution, etc.

INDIVIDUAL WORK

1. Keep a notebook to record information from daily lectures.
2. Read one fiction and one nonfiction account of the Revolution. Respond to the passages.
3. Write a research paper about a man or woman from any country who contributed to the Revolution. Use one primary source, one secondary source, and one Internet source to write the paper.

METHODS OF ASSESSMENT

1. Checklist for notebook
2. Rubric for written responses to literature
3. Rubric for group project
4. Checklist for research paper
5. Rubric for research paper

Thank you to Jennie Buck (Wheeler Elementary, Speedway Schools, Indiana) for providing the ideas for this performance task.
(*Standards adapted from Indiana Department of Education. [n.d.]. *Indiana academic standards.* Retrieved March 10, 2004, from http://www.indianastandards.org/)

▪ AMERICAN REVOLUTION CHECKLIST 1 ▪

COURSE/CLASS _Social studies_   GRADE _5_

STANDARD* _Language Arts 5.4.5: Use note-taking skills._

ACTIVITY _Keep a notebook to record information from daily lectures._

CRITERIA/PERFORMANCE INDICATORS	Not Yet [0]	Some Evidence [1]
Organization		
● I used headings to identify topics.		
● I dated all my entries.		
● I skipped lines when I switched topics.		
● I have ordered all my entries sequentially, by date.		
Completeness		
● I took notes for all classroom lectures.		
Neatness		
● I can read my own handwriting.		
● A friend can read my handwriting.		
● The teacher can read my handwriting.		
Timeliness		
● I handed in my notebook on time.		

COMMENTS

Scale

9	=	A
8	=	B
7	=	C
6	=	D
0–5	=	F

Thank you to Jennie Buck (Wheeler Elementary, Speedway Schools, Indiana) for providing the ideas for this checklist. (*Standard from Indiana Department of Education. [n.d.]. *Indiana academic standards.* Retrieved March 10, 2004, from http://www.indianastandards.org/)

▪ AMERICAN REVOLUTION CHECKLIST 2 ▪

COURSE/CLASS _Social Studies_   **GRADE** _5_

STANDARDS* _Social Studies 5.1.13: Assess the influence of other countries, such as France, Spain, Russia, Germany, Poland, and the Netherlands, in the American Revolution; identify individuals from other countries who assisted the American cause. 5.1.14: Identify and evaluate contributions of women during the American Revolution, including Abigail Adams, Martha Washington, Mercy Otis Warren, and Molly Pitcher. 5.1.20: Read historical fiction and nonfiction about an event of the American Revolution and reconstruct the literal meaning of passages by identifying who was involved, what happened, where it happened, what events led to these developments, and what consequences or outcomes followed._

**Language Arts** 5.5.2: Write responses to literature that demonstrate an understanding of a literary work, support judgments through references to the text and to prior knowledge, and develop interpretations that exhibit careful reading and under-standing. 5.5.3: Write research reports about important ideas, issues, or events by using the following guidelines: frame ques-tions that direct the investigation; establish a main idea or topic; develop the topic with simple facts, details, examples, and explanations; and use a variety of information sources, including firsthand interviews, reference materials, and electronic resources, to locate information for the report.

ACTIVITY _Write a research paper about a man or woman from any country who contributed to the Revolution. Use one pri-mary source, one secondary source, and one Internet source to write the paper._

CRITERIA/PERFORMANCE INDICATORS	Not Yet [0]	Some Evidence [1]
Establish a Topic		
• I have chosen a topic relating to the Revolutionary War.		
• I have developed 3 questions about my topic.		
Collection of Sources		
• I have at least 1 primary source.		
• I have at least 1 secondary source.		
• I have at least 1 Internet source.		
Topic Development		
• Each question has at least 3 answers (facts or details).		
• Information from all 3 sources has been included.		
Bibliography		
• I listed my sources in alphabetical order by title.		
• I followed the correct format.		

COMMENTS

Scale

9	=	A
8	=	B
7	=	C
6	=	D
0–5	=	F

Thank you to Jennie Buck (Wheeler Elementary, Speedway City Schools, Indiana) for providing the ideas for this rubric. (*Standards from Indiana Department of Education. [n.d.]. _Indiana academic standards._ Retrieved March 10, 2004, from http://www.indianastandards.org/)

▪ AMERICAN REVOLUTION RUBRIC ▪

COURSE/CLASS _Social Studies_   GRADE _5_

STANDARDS* _LA 5.5.3: Write a research report about ideas, issues, or events. LA 5.6.3, 5.6.5, 5.6.6, 5.6.7: Writing conventions. SS 5.1.12, 5.1.14: Identify contributions of leaders and women. SS 5.1.13: Assess influences of other countries._

SS 5.1.20: Reconstruct an event, including outcomes and consequences.

ACTIVITY _Write a research paper about a man or woman from any country who contributed to the Revolution. Use one primary source, one secondary source, and one Internet source to write the paper._

SCORING / CRITERIA	1 Below Standards	2 Almost Meets Standards	3 Meets Standards	4 Exceeds Standards	SCORE
TOPIC • Topic is guided by specific questions posed before research begins. • Topic is well developed with details, examples, and explanations of the research.	• No questions posed. • Research is incomplete.	• Topic is guided by 1 or 2 questions. • Topic is underdeveloped; details, examples, and explanations of the research are missing.	• Topic is guided by specific questions posed before research begins. • Topic is well developed with details, examples, and explanations of the research.	• Topic is guided by specific questions posed before research begins. Questions are insightful and inventive. • Topic is well developed with details, examples, and explanations of the research. Examples and details are extraordinary and interesting.	__ x 5 = ___ (20) __ x 5 = ___ (20)
CONTENT • The person's importance is explained in the introduction. • The person's influence is detailed in the body of the paper. • The consequences of the person's contributions are addressed in the conclusion.	• No person's importance is explained in the introduction. • No person's influence is detailed in the body of the paper. • None of the consequences are addressed in the conclusion.	• The person's importance is inaccurately explained in the introduction. • The person's influence is inaccurately detailed in the body of the paper. • The consequences of the person's contributions are inaccurately addressed in the conclusion.	• The person's importance is explained in the introduction. • The person's influence is detailed in the body of the paper. • The consequences of the person's contributions are addressed in the conclusion.	• The person's importance is explained in the introduction. Unique insights into the person's importance are included. • The person's influence is detailed in the body of the paper. Special insights into the person's influence are included. • The consequences of the person's contributions are addressed in the conclusion. Little-known contributions are explained.	__ x 10 = ___ (40) __ x 10 = ___ (40) __ x 10 = ___ (40)
CONVENTIONS • Correct capitalization is used. • Correct punctuation is used. • Verbs in past tense are used consistently throughout the paper. • Correct spelling is used.	• Many capitalization mistakes are made. • Numerous punctuation mistakes are made. • Verb tenses are used inconsistently throughout the paper. • Many spelling errors are made.	• Some capitalization mistakes are made. • Some punctuation mistakes are made. • Verbs in past tense are used inconsistently throughout the paper. • Some spelling errors are made.	• Only 1 capitalization error made. • Only 1 punctuation error made. • Verbs in past tense are used consistently throughout the paper; only 1 or 2 mistakes in tense are made. • Only 1 spelling error is made.	• Correct capitalization is used. • Correct punctuation is used. • Verbs in past tense are used consistently throughout the paper. • Correct spelling is used.	__ x 5 = ___ (20) __ x 5 = ___ (20) __ x 5 = ___ (20) __ x 5 = ___ (20)

COMMENTS:

216–240	=	A
192–215	=	B
168–191	=	C
144–167	=	D
0–143	=	F

Final Score _____/(240)

Final Grade _____

Thank you to Jennie Buck (Wheeler Elementary, Speedway City Schools, Indiana) for providing the ideas for this rubric. (*Standards from Indiana Department of Education. [n.d.]. _Indiana academic standards_. Retrieved March 10, 2004, from http://www.indianastandards.org/)

Example

Family Fitness Night

❏ Performance Task

❏ Checklist

❏ Rubric

▪ FAMILY FITNESS NIGHT PERFORMANCE TASK ▪

COURSE/CLASS _Physical Education_   GRADE _7_

STANDARDS* _7.4.1: Utilize self-assessment of physical fitness to identify strengths and weaknesses and use this information to develop a personalized fitness program. Example: Develop fitness program that addresses all of the components (parts) of fitness. 7.4.2: Demonstrate an understanding of the importance of maintaining all components (parts) of fitness at a high level. Example: Participate in preactivity stretching exercise to improve flexibility and to prepare for the activity. 7.4.3: Demonstrate an understanding of the concepts of health-related (healthy lifestyle) fitness and apply these concepts in various physical activities. Example: Use target heart rate to monitor the intensity of aerobic (heart and lung enhancing) activities._

TASK DESCRIPTION

You have been selected by the National Fitness Association to design a Family Fitness Night for the community. The project includes researching the seven components of fitness, designing exercises for each component, providing a written explanation of the exercises, making posters to invite people to the fitness event, and creating a portfolio for this physical fitness unit.

DIRECT INSTRUCTION FOR WHOLE CLASS   The whole class will be involved in the following learning experience:

1. _Listen to a lecture about and discuss the seven components of fitness._
2. _Take a field trip to the National Institute of Fitness and Sport._
3. _Review expectations for the graphics and information to be included on the posters._

GROUP WORK

Group One	Group Two	Group Three	Group Four	Group Five
Research one component of fitness: endurance. Demonstrate exercises for this component and write an explanation of the exercises.	_Research one component of fitness: strength. Demonstrate exercises for this component and write an explanation of the exercises._	_Research two components of fitness: speed and agility. Demonstrate exercises for these components and write an explanation of the exercises._	_Research one component of fitness: flexibility. Demonstrate exercises for this component and provide a written explanation of the exercises._	_Research two components of fitness: balance and coordination. Demonstrate exercises for these components and write an explanation of the exercises._

INDIVIDUAL WORK

1. _Prepare a poster that advertises the Family Fitness Night._
2. _Compile a portfolio that includes selected assignments, performance tests, and student reflections on each component._

METHODS OF ASSESSMENT

1. _Checklist for group project_
2. _Rubric for group project_
3. _Checklist for poster_
4. _Checklist for portfolio_
5. _Rubric for portfolio_
6. _Teacher-made test on the components of fitness_

Thank you to Clara Caito (Fisher Elementary School, Speedway City Schools, Indiana) and Terrie Maexner (Ben Davis Jr. High School, MSD of Wayne Township, Indiana) for providing the ideas for this performance task. (*Standards adapted from Indiana Department of Education. [n.d.]. _Indiana academic standards._ Retrieved March 11, 2004, from http://www.indianastandards.org/)

▪ FAMILY FITNESS NIGHT CHECKLIST 1 ▪

COURSE/CLASS _Physical Education_   **GRADE** _7_

STANDARDS* _7.4.1: Utilize self-assessment of physical fitness to identify strengths and weaknesses and use this information to develop a personalized fitness program. Example: Develop fitness program that addresses all of the components (parts) of fitness. 7.4.2: Demonstrate an understanding of the importance of maintaining all components (parts) of fitness at a high level. Example: Participate in preactivity stretching exercise to improve flexibility and to prepare for the activity._

7.4.3: Demonstrate an understanding of the concepts of health-related (healthy lifestyle) fitness and apply these concepts in various physical activities. Example: Use target heart rate to monitor the intensity of aerobic (heart and lung enhancing) activities.

ACTIVITY _Group project on fitness component(s)._

CRITERIA/PERFORMANCE INDICATORS	Not Yet [0]	Some Evidence [1]
Organization of Information		
• What is the fitness component?		
• What activities will help a person improve on this component?		
• Why is this component important?		
Work Habits		
• Complete work on time		
• Work well with the group		
• Ask for help when needed		
• Self-motivated		
Readability		
• Use proper grammar		
• Include specific information		
• Include clear and concise explanation		
Knowledge of Fitness Component		
• Develop exercises specific to the component		
• Demonstrate exercises specific to the component		
• Explain the exercises		

COMMENTS

Scale

12–13	=	A
10–11	=	B
9	=	C
8	=	D
0–7	=	F

Thank you to Clara Caito (Fisher Elementary School, Speedway City Schools, Indiana) and Terrie Maexner (Ben Davis Jr. High School, MSD of Wayne Township, Indiana) for providing the ideas for this checklist. (*Standards adapted from Indiana Department of Education. [n.d.]. _Indiana academic standards._ Retrieved March 11, 2004, from http://www.indianastandards.org/)

▪ FAMILY FITNESS NIGHT CHECKLIST 2 ▪

COURSE/CLASS _Physical Education_   **GRADE** _7_

STANDARDS* _7.4.1: Utilize self-assessment of physical fitness to identify strengths and weaknesses and use this information to develop a personalized fitness program. Example: Develop fitness program that addresses all of the components (parts) of fitness. 7.4.2: Demonstrate an understanding of the importance of maintaining all components (parts) of fitness at a high level. Example: Participate in pre-activity stretching exercise to improve flexibility and to prepare for the activity._

7.4.3: Demonstrate an understanding of the concepts of health-related (healthy lifestyle) fitness and apply these concepts in various physical activities. Example: Use target heart rate to monitor the intensity of aerobic (heart and lung enhancing) activities.

ACTIVITY _Prepare a poster that advertises the Family Fitness Night._

CRITERIA/PERFORMANCE INDICATORS	Not Yet [0]	Some Evidence [1]
Work Habits		
● Complete work on time		
● Ask for help when needed		
● Self-motivated		
Creativity		
● Colorful		
● Informative		
● Detailed		
● Unique		
Organization of Information		
● Who is invited?		
● What is the Family Fitness Night?		
● When is the Family Fitness Night?		
● Where is the Family Fitness Night?		
● Why should people attend?		
Readability		
● Use proper grammar		
● Include specific information		
● Visually appealing		

COMMENTS

Scale

14–15	=	A
12–13	=	B
11	=	C
10	=	D
0–9	=	F

Thank you to Clara Caito (Fisher Elementary School, Speedway City Schools, Indiana) and Terrie Maexner (Ben Davis Jr. High School, MSD of Wayne Township, Indiana) for providing the ideas for this checklist. (*Standards adapted from Indiana Department of Education. [n.d.]. Indiana academic standards. Retrieved March 11, 2004, from http://www.indianastandards.org/)

▪ FAMILY FITNESS NIGHT RUBRIC ▪

COURSE/CLASS _Physical Education_   **GRADE** _7_

STANDARDS* _7.4.1: Utilize self-assessment of physical fitness to identify strengths and weaknesses and use this information to develop a personalized fitness program. 7.4.2: Demonstrate an understanding of the importance of maintaining all components (parts) of fitness at a high level. 7.4.3: Demonstrate an understanding of the concepts of health-related (healthy lifestyle) fitness and apply these concepts in various physical activities._

ACTIVITY _Compile a portfolio that includes selected assignments, performance tests, and student reflections on each component._

SCORING CRITERIA	1 Below Standards	2 Almost Meets Standards	3 Meets Standards	4 Exceeds Standards	SCORE
VISUAL APPEAL • Cover • Artwork for exercises • Neatness	Missing 2 elements	Missing 1 element	All 3 elements included	All 3 elements are creatively and visually appealing	___ x 5 = ___ (20)
FORM • Spelling • Grammar • Sentence structure	4–6 errors	1–3 errors	No errors	No errors; high level of writing skills	___ x 5 = ___ (20)
ORGANIZATION • Table of contents • 7 components included • Timeliness	Missing 2 elements	Missing 1 element	All 3 elements included	All 3 elements demonstrate a high level of organization	___ x 5 = ___ (20)
REFLECTIONS • 1 reflection per component • Depth of reflections • Self-assessment	Missing 2 or more reflections	Missing 1 reflection	All 7 reflections are complete and thought provoking	All 7 reflections are thought provoking and show the ability to self-assess	___ x 5 = ___ (20)
KNOWLEDGE OF KEY CONCEPTS • Fitness components • Evidence of understanding • Application of each component	Little evidence of understanding of key concepts	Evidence of basic understanding of key concepts	Evidence of high level understanding of key concepts	Evidence of the ability to apply knowledge to new situations	___ x 5 = ___ (20)

COMMENTS:

95–100 = A	
88–94 = B	Final Score _____/(100)
77–87 = C	
70–76 = D	Final Grade _____
0–69 = F	

Thank you to Clara Caito (Fisher Elementary School, Speedway City Schools, Indiana) and Terrie Maexner (Ben Davis Jr. High School, MSD of Wayne Township, Indiana) for providing the ideas for this rubric. (*Standards adapted from Indiana Department of Education. [n.d.]. _Indiana academic standards._ Retrieved March 11, 2004, from http://www.indianastandards.org/)

Example

September 11

❑ Performance Task

❑ Checklist

❑ Rubric

▪ SEPTEMBER 11 PERFORMANCE TASK ▪

COURSE/CLASS _Mathematics_   **GRADE** _7_

STANDARDS* _7.2.2: Calculate the percentage increase and decrease of a quantity._

7.6.1: Analyze, interpret, and display data in appropriate bar, line, and circle graphs and stem-and-leaf plots and justify the choice of display.

**Language Arts** 7.6: Writing, English language conventions: Students write using standard English conventions (sentence structure, grammar, punctuation, capitalization, and spelling) appropriate to the grade level.

TASK DESCRIPTION

There is considerable concern regarding the impact of the tragic events of September 11, 2001. Because of your expert math and data analysis abilities, you have been selected by the governor to serve on a citizens' committee to investigate the economic impact this event had on Indiana. You will gather data from multiple criteria from before and after September 11, 2001, and calculate the percent of change for each criterion. Your information should be displayed on a spreadsheet and a graph of your choice. You will present your findings to the governor on March 30.

DIRECT INSTRUCTION FOR WHOLE CLASS | The whole class will be involved in the following learning experience:

1. _Learn how to convert any two representations of numbers (fractions, decimals, percents)._
2. _Discover how to calculate the percent of change._
3. _Learn how to create a spreadsheet._
4. _Discover how to choose the best type of graph to use to display data._
5. _Learn how to create a graph from a spreadsheet._

GROUP WORK

Group One	Group Two	Group Three	Group Four
Gather data about home ownership (e.g., mortgage interest rates, mortgage defaults, new building permits) from before and after September 11, 2001, and calculate the percent of change for each criterion. Display the information on a spreadsheet and a graph of your choice.	_Gather data about travel (e.g., amount of air travel, amount of land travel [bus, train, car], money spent on travel, travel-related security, cancellation of tickets purchased before 9-11) from before and after September 11, 2001, and calculate the percent of change for each criterion. Display the information on a spreadsheet and a graph of your choice._	_Gather data about entertainment (e.g., movie theater ticket sales, restaurant revenue, video rentals) from before and after September 11, 2001, and calculate the percent of change for each criterion. Display the information on a spreadsheet and a graph of your choice._	_Gather data about employment (e.g., number of unemployed, number of people on welfare, number of people on Medicare) from before and after September 11, 2001, and calculate the percent of change for each criterion. Display the information on a spreadsheet and a graph of your choice._

INDIVIDUAL WORK

1. _Before working on group projects, each student should complete worksheets on converting fractions and decimals into percents._
2. _Before working on group projects, each student should complete worksheets on calculating the percent of change._
3. _After working on group projects, each student should complete a reflection essay that discusses his or her feelings about what the statistics show._

METHODS OF ASSESSMENT

1. _Checklist for group project_
2. _Rubric to assess reflection essay_
3. _Teacher-made test on percent of change_

Thank you to Judith Schmidt (Craig Middle School, MSD of Warren Township, Indiana) for providing the ideas for this performance task. (*Standards from Indiana Department of Education. [n.d.]. _Indiana academic standards_. Retrieved March 11, 2004, from http://www.indianastandards.org/)

▪ SEPTEMBER 11 CHECKLIST ▪

COURSE/CLASS _Mathematics_   **GRADE** _7_

STANDARDS* _**Mathematics** 7.2.2: Calculate the percentage increase and decrease of a quantity._
7.6.1: Analyze, interpret, and display data in appropriate bar, line, and circle graphs and stem-and-leaf plots and justify the choice of display.
**Language Arts** 7.6: Writing, English language conventions: Students write using standard English conventions (sentence structure, grammar, punctuation, capitalization, and spelling) appropriate to the grade level.

ACTIVITY _Group project on data before and after September 11, 2001. Project includes calculation of percentage of change for several criteria, a spreadsheet, and a graph of group's choice._

CRITERIA/PERFORMANCE INDICATORS	Not Yet [0]	Yes [1]
Spreadsheet		
● Appropriate criteria used		
● Multiple criteria used		
● Data from before 9-11 included		
● Data from after 9-11 included		
● Percent of change calculated correctly for each criterion		
Graph		
● Correct type of graph chosen to show change		
● Title included		
● Parts of graph labeled		
● Graph is accurate		
● Graph is neat and readable		
Group Effort		
● Worked cooperatively in group		
● Handed in work by due date		

COMMENTS

Scale

11–12	=	A
9–10	=	B
8	=	C
7	=	D
0–6	=	F

Thank you to Judith Schmidt (Craig Middle School, MSD of Warren Township, Indiana) for providing the ideas for this performance task. (*Standards from Indiana Department of Education. [n.d.]. _Indiana academic standards._ Retrieved March 11, 2004, from http://www.indianastandards.org/)

■ SEPTEMBER 11 RUBRIC ■

COURSE/CLASS _Mathematics_   **GRADE** _7_

STANDARDS* _Mathematics 7.2.2: Calculate the percentage increase and decrease of a quantity._

7.6.1: Analyze, interpret, and display data in appropriate bar, line, and circle graphs and stem-and-leaf plots and justify the choice of display.

Language Arts 7.6: Writing, English language conventions: Students write using standard English conventions (sentence structure, grammar, punctuation, capitalization, and spelling) appropriate to the grade level.

ACTIVITY _After working on group projects, each student should complete a reflection essay that discusses his or her feelings about what the statistics show._

SCORING / CRITERIA	1 Below Standards	2 Almost Meets Standards	3 Meets Standards	4 Exceeds Standards	SCORE
WRITING DEVELOPMENT • Focus	• Provides little or no focus on topic and task	• Stays somewhat focused on topic and task	• Stays mostly focused on topic and task but sometimes rambles and repeats	• Stays focused on topic and task and does not ramble or repeat	__ x 5 = __ (20)
• Relevant ideas and information	• Includes minimal relevant ideas and little information	• Includes few relevant ideas and information	• Includes relevant ideas and information	• Includes thorough, complete, and relevant ideas and information	__ x 5 = __ (20)
• Order	• Exhibits little or no order	• Provides some order but may be missing a beginning, a middle, or an end	• Uses orderly progression but may show 1 or 2 lapses in order	• Follows a clear order with a beginning, a middle, and an end	__ x 5 = __ (20)
• Vocabulary	• Exhibits limited vocabulary	• Exhibits minimal vocabulary usage	• Exhibits adequate vocabulary usage	• Exhibits exceptional vocabulary usage	__ x 5 = __ (20)
• Clarity of ideas	• Does not express ideas clearly; ideas are not apparent	• Does not express ideas clearly; ideas are apparent but unclear	• Expresses ideas clearly	• Expresses ideas clearly; work is fluid and easy to read	__ x 5 = __ (20)
LANGUAGE USE • Capitalization	• Many capitalization errors	• Frequent errors in capitalization	• Most capitalization correct	• No capitalization errors	__ x 5 = __ (20)
• Punctuation	• Many punctuation errors	• Frequent errors in punctuation	• Most punctuation correct	• No punctuation errors	__ x 5 = __ (20)
• Spelling	• Many spelling errors	• Frequent errors in spelling	• Most spelling correct	• No spelling errors	__ x 5 = __ (20)
• Grammar and word usage	• Many grammar and word usage errors	• Frequent errors in grammar and word usage	• Most grammar and word usage correct	• No errors in grammar or word usage	__ x 5 = __ (20)
• Paragraphing	• Many paragraphing errors	• Frequent errors in paragraphing	• Most paragraphing correct	• No errors in paragraphing	__ x 5 = __ (20)
• Run-on sentences and sentence fragments	• Many run-on sentences or sentence fragments	• Frequent run-on sentences or sentence fragments	• Few run-on sentences or sentence fragments	• No run-on sentences or sentence fragments	__ x 5 = __ (20)

COMMENTS

198–220	=	A
176–197	=	B
154–175	=	C
132–153	=	D
0–131	=	F

Final Score   ___/(220)

Final Grade   _____

Thank you to Judith Schmidt (Craig Middle School, MSD of Warren Township, Indiana) for providing the ideas for this performance task. (*Standards from Indiana Department of Education. [n.d.]. _Indiana academic standards._ Retrieved March 11, 2004, from http://www.indianastandards.org/)

Example

Martin Luther King, Jr.

❏ Performance Task

❏ Checklist

❏ Rubric

■ MARTIN LUTHER KING, JR. PERFORMANCE TASK ■

COURSE/CLASS _Language Arts_   **GRADE** _7_

STANDARDS* _7.5: Writing, applications: Students continue to write narrative (story), expository (informational), persuasive, and descriptive texts. Students are introduced to writing biographical and autobiographical narratives, responses to literature, research reports, persuasive compositions, and summaries of grade-level-appropriate reading materials. The writing demonstrates a command of standard English and research, organizational, and drafting strategies. Writing demonstrates an awareness of the audience (intended reader) and purpose for writing._

7.6: Writing, English language conventions: Students write using standard English conventions (sentence structure, grammar, punctuation, capitalization, and spelling) appropriate to the grade level.

TASK DESCRIPTION

You have been asked by the Indianapolis chapter of the NAACP to prepare a presentation to educate middle school students on the importance of commemorating Martin Luther King, Jr. Your presentation should include an oral recitation and interpretation of the "I Have a Dream" speech. Each group will focus on one of the following topics: Martin Luther King, Jr.'s thoughts and feelings revealed in the speech, underlying causes behind the speech, the "check" referred to in the speech, or comparing the world or country in the 1960s to our world or country today. You will give your presentation on February 14.

DIRECT INSTRUCTION FOR WHOLE CLASS | The whole class will be involved in the following learning experience:

1. Listen and read along as a recording of Dr. King's "I Have a Dream" speech is played.
2. Answer recall questions about the main ideas in each paragraph of the speech.
3. Examine different types of graphic organizers and review outlines.

GROUP WORK

Group One	Group Two	Group Three	Group Four
Create a presentation on Martin Luther King Jr.'s thoughts and feelings revealed in the "I Have a Dream" speech. Work together to evaluate each group member's individual essay (see Individual Work).	Create a presentation on the underlying causes behind the "I Have a Dream" speech. Work together to evaluate each group member's individual essay (see Individual Work).	Create a presentation on the "check" referred to in the "I Have a Dream" speech. Work together to evaluate each group member's individual essay (see Individual Work).	Create a presentation that compares the world or country in the 1960s to the world or country today. (Be sure to use quotes from the "I Have a Dream" speech to back up your claims.) Work together to evaluate each group member's individual essay (see Individual Work).

INDIVIDUAL WORK

1. Prepare a graphic organizer or outline for your group's topic.
2. Write an essay directly related to your organizer or outline. Your essay should be more than 100 words long.
3. Prepare a visual promoting a commemoration day for Martin Luther King, Jr.

METHODS OF ASSESSMENT

1. Checklists (individual and group) for essay
2. Rubric to assess essay
3. Rubric to assess visual promoting a commemoration for Martin Luther King, Jr.

Thank you to Leslie F. Knox (Stonybrook Middle School, MSD of Warren Township, Indiana) for providing the ideas for this performance task. (*Standards adapted from Indiana Department of Education. [n.d.]. _Indiana academic standards._ Retrieved March 11, 2004, from http://www.indianastandards.org/)

■ MARTIN LUTHER KING, JR. CHECKLIST 1 ■

COURSE/CLASS _Language Arts_   **GRADE** _7_

STANDARDS* _7.5: Writing, applications: Students continue to write narrative (story), expository (informational), persuasive, and descriptive texts. Students are introduced to writing biographical and autobiographical narratives, responses to literature, research reports, persuasive compositions, and summaries of grade-level-appropriate reading materials. The writing demonstrates a command of standard English and research, organizational, and drafting strategies. Writing demonstrates an awareness of the audience (intended reader) and purpose for writing._

7.6: Writing, English language conventions: Students write using standard English conventions (sentence structure, grammar, punctuation, capitalization, and spelling) appropriate to the grade level.

ACTIVITY _Create a graphic organizer or outline for your group's topic and write an essay directly related to the organizer or outline. The essay should be more than 100 words long. Note: The following checklist is to be used by individual students to evaluate their own essays._

CRITERIA/PERFORMANCE INDICATORS	Not Yet [0]	Yes [1]
Blue or black ink		
Secondary heading		
Neatness (no folds in paper, neat corrections)		
Graphic organizer or outline		
Essay written directly from organizer or outline		
Spelling: few errors		
Grammar: subject-verb agreement		
Grammar: correct indefinite pronouns		
Capitalization		
Punctuation: series commas		
Punctuation: commas in compound sentences		
Sentence structure: 1 compound sentence		
Sentence structure: 1 complex sentence		
Thesis statement		
Support (minimum of 3 supporting statements from text)		
Visual		

COMMENTS

Scale

14–16	=	A
11–12	=	B
10–11	=	C
9	=	D
0–8	=	F

Thank you to Leslie F. Knox (Stonybrook Middle School, MSD of Warren Township, Indiana) for providing the ideas for this performance task. (*Standards adapted from Indiana Department of Education. [n.d.]. _Indiana academic standards._ Retrieved March 11, 2004, from http://www.indianastandards.org/)

■ MARTIN LUTHER KING, JR. CHECKLIST 2 ■

COURSE/CLASS _Language Arts_   GRADE _7_

STANDARDS* _7.5: Writing, applications: Students continue to write narrative (story), expository (informational), persuasive, and descriptive texts. Students are introduced to writing biographical and autobiographical narratives, responses to literature, research reports, persuasive compositions, and summaries of grade-level-appropriate reading materials. The writing demonstrates a command of standard English and research, organizational, and drafting strategies. Writing demonstrates an awareness of the audience (intended reader) and purpose for writing._

7.6: Writing, English language conventions: Students write using standard English conventions (sentence structure, grammar, punctuation, capitalization, and spelling) appropriate to the grade level.

ACTIVITY _Create a graphic organizer or outline for your group's topic and write an essay directly related to the organizer or outline. The essay should be more than 100 words long. Note: The following checklist is to be used by students in each group to evaluate their fellow group members' essays. Each student in the group is responsible to proofread all of the group members' essays in one of the following areas: spelling, grammar, capitalization, punctuation, and sentence structure. The teacher will check the thesis statement and support, as well as the visual._

CRITERIA/PERFORMANCE INDICATORS	Student 1: ___(name)	Student 2: ___(name)	Student 3: ___(name)	Student 4: ___(name)	Student 5: ___(name)
Spelling: few errors	__yes __no	__yes __no	__yes __no	__yes __no	__yes __no
Grammar: subject-verb agreement and correct indefinite pronouns	__yes __no	__yes __no	__yes __no	__yes __no	__yes __no
Capitalization: few errors	__yes __no	__yes __no	__yes __no	__yes __no	__yes __no
Punctuation: series commas and commas in compound sentences	__yes __no	__yes __no	__yes __no	__yes __no	__yes __no
Sentence structure: 1 compound sentence and 1 complex sentence	__yes __no	__yes __no	__yes __no	__yes __no	__yes __no
Thesis statement and support: minimum of 3 supporting statements from text	__yes __no	__yes __no	__yes __no	__yes __no	__yes __no
Visual	__yes __no	__yes __no	__yes __no	__yes __no	__yes __no

COMMENTS

Thank you to Leslie F. Knox (Stonybrook Middle School, MSD of Warren Township, Indiana) for providing the ideas for this performance task. (*Standards adapted from Indiana Department of Education. [n.d.]. _Indiana academic standards._ Retrieved March 11, 2004, from http://www.indianastandards.org/)

■ MARTIN LUTHER KING, JR. RUBRIC ■

COURSE/CLASS _Language Arts_   **GRADE** _7_

STANDARDS* _7.5: Writing, applications: Students continue to write narrative (story), expository (informational), persuasive, and descriptive texts. Students are introduced to writing biographical and autobiographical narratives, responses to literature, research reports, persuasive compositions, and summaries of grade-level-appropriate reading materials. The writing demonstrates a command of standard English and research, organizational, and drafting strategies. Writing demonstrates an awareness of the audience (intended reader) and purpose for writing._

7.6: Writing, English language conventions: Students write using standard English conventions (sentence structure, grammar, punctuation, capitalization, and spelling) appropriate to the grade level.

ACTIVITY _Create a graphic organizer or outline for your group's topic and write an essay directly related to the organizer or outline. The essay should be more than 100 words long._

SCORING / CRITERIA	1 Below Standards	2 Almost Meets Standards	3 Meets Standards	4 Exceeds Standards	SCORE
DIRECTIONS • Correct heading • Blue or black ink • Left and right margins • Neat	• 1 element follows directions	• 2 elements follow directions	• 3 elements follow directions	• All elements follow directions	___ x 5 = ___ (20)
CONTENT • Addresses topics • Thesis statement • Minimum of 3 supporting details	• 1 element supports content	• 2 elements support content	• 3 elements support content	• All elements support content	___ x 5 = ___ (20)
ORGANIZATION • Outline followed • Correct paragraphing used • Cohesive order (beginning, middle, end)	• 1 element supports organization	• 2 elements support organization	• 3 elements support organization	• All elements support organization	___ x 5 = ___ (20)
STRUCTURE • Subject-verb agreement • Correct indefinite pronouns used • 1 complex sentence • 1 compound sentence	• 1 structural element correct	• 2 structural elements correct	• 3 structural elements correct	• All structural elements correct	___ x 5 = ___ (20)
MECHANICS • Capitalization • Commas • Spelling	• 4 or more errors	• 2 or 3 errors	• 1 error	• No errors	___ x 5 = ___ (20)

COMMENTS

90–100 = A	
80–89 = B	Final Score _____/(100)
70–79 = C	
60–69 = D	Final Grade _____
0–59 = F	

Thank you to Leslie F. Knox (Stonybrook Middle School, MSD of Warren Township, Indiana) for providing the ideas for this performance task. (*Standards adapted from Indiana Department of Education. [n.d.]. _Indiana academic standards._ Retrieved March 11, 2004, from http://www.indianastandards.org/)

Example

Spanish Children's Book

❏ Performance Task

❏ Checklist

❏ Rubric

■ SPANISH CHILDREN'S BOOK PERFORMANCE TASK ■

COURSE/CLASS _Spanish_   **GRADE** _High School, Level 4_

STANDARDS* _4.3: Students present information, concepts, and ideas to an audience of listeners or readers on a variety of topics. (Presentational)_

4.3.2: Produce and/or present elaborate creative works. Example: Create short written pieces such as children's books or travel brochures.

TASK DESCRIPTION

Our class has been asked by the ENL (English as a New Language) director for our district to buddy up with their Spanish-speaking students for a mutually powerful learning opportunity. You will kick off this endeavor by writing and illustrating a children's storybook in Spanish. You will read your book to a small group of 3 to 5 Spanish-speaking students. Then you will assist your audience as they retell the story in English.

DIRECT INSTRUCTION FOR WHOLE CLASS The whole class will be involved in the following learning experience:

1. Read and discuss a variety of children's books in Spanish, noting elements of a well-written children's story.
2. Practice constructing sentences using proper grammar.
3. After stories are written, do a peer review of stories before sharing stories with Spanish-speaking students.
4. Review social skills to prepare for working with younger students.
5. Brainstorm and discuss possible settings for a children's story (cultures, civilizations, countries, etc.).

GROUP WORK

Group One	Group Two	Group Three	Group Four
Do research on the ancient Aztec civilization.	Do research on modern-day Mexico City.	Do research on a modern-day village in Latin America.	Do research on a modern-day island country in the Caribbean.

INDIVIDUAL WORK

1. Write a children's book in Spanish about the civilization, city, village, or country you researched with your group. Be sure to illustrate your story.
2. Share the book with a small group of 3 to 5 Spanish-speaking students. Assist your group to retell the story in English.
3. Optional extension activity: Write a letter to a publisher explaining the value of your book. Tell the publisher why it should be published and why people would purchase it. Describe the highlights of the book.

METHODS OF ASSESSMENT

1. Checklists for presentation
2. Rubric for book
3. Self-assessment of book, presentation, and process (reflection)

Thank you to Jennifer Hasler (Westfield High School, Indiana) for providing the ideas for this performance task. (*Standards adapted from Indiana Department of Education. [n.d.]. _Indiana academic standards._ Retrieved March 11, 2004, from http://www.indianastandards.org/)

▪ SPANISH CHILDREN'S BOOK CHECKLIST ▪

COURSE/CLASS _Spanish_   **GRADE** _High School, Level 4_

STANDARDS* _4.3: Students present information, concepts, and ideas to an audience of listeners or readers on a variety_
of topics. (Presentational)
4.3.2: Produce and/or present elaborate creative works. Example: Create short written pieces
such as children's books or travel brochures.

ACTIVITY _Present your Spanish children's storybook to a small group of 3 to 5 Spanish-speaking students. Assist your audience_
as they retell the story in English.

CRITERIA/PERFORMANCE INDICATORS	Not Yet [0]	Yes [1]
Organization		
• Correct vocabulary		
• Complete sentences		
• Correct verb conjugations		
Delivery of Presentation		
• Enthusiasm		
• Clear speech		
• Good posture and eye contact		
• Appropriate props and attire		
Teamwork		
• Incorporate notes from peer review		
• Peer edit others' work		
• Listen to other presentations		
• Collaborate with team planning		
• Collaborate with team during presentation		

COMMENTS

Scale

11–12	=	A
10	=	B
9	=	C
8	=	D
0–7	=	F

Thank you to Jennifer Hasler (Westfield High School, Indiana) for providing the ideas for this checklist. (*Standards adapted from Indiana Department of Education. [n.d.]. _Indiana academic standards._ Retrieved March 11, 2004, from http://www.indianastandards.org/)

▪ SPANISH CHILDREN'S BOOK RUBRIC ▪

COURSE/CLASS *Spanish*   **GRADE** *High School, Level 4*

STANDARDS*   *4.3: Students present information, concepts, and ideas to an audience of listeners or readers on a variety of topics. (Presentational)*

4.3.2: Produce and/or present elaborate creative works. Example: Create short written pieces such as children's books or travel brochures.

ACTIVITY *Write a children's book in Spanish about the civilization, city, village, or country you researched with your group. Be sure to illustrate your story.*

SCORING CRITERIA	1 Below Standards	2 Almost Meets Standards	3 Meets Standards	4 Exceeds Standards	SCORE
STORY HOLDS INTEREST OF YOUR AUDIENCE • Vocabulary • Pictures and graphics accompany storyline • Colorful, interesting protagonist solves a problem or remedies a situation	• Uses 5 or more phrases that are not understood by audience • Less than $1/2$ of book is illustrated; pictures haphazardly follow storyline • Loses audience; their minds wander	• Vocabulary appropriate; fails to introduce words to extend vocabulary words • Several pictures throughout book, but many are irrelevant to story or lack color • Audience is confused	• Vocabulary appropriate; uses new words but does not explain them • Colorful, relevant pictures on each page • Audience engaged most of the time; confusions are explained	• Vocabulary appropriate; extends vocabulary by introducing and explaining new words • More than 1 colorful, relevant picture per page • Audience couldn't wait to hear more; they're hanging on your every word	___ x 5 = ___ (20) ___ x 5 = ___ (20) ___ x 5 = ___ (20)
STORY INTENSITY • Problem • Solution • Setting • Characters	• Main character's problem is unclear • No solution offered or solution was not understood • Setting is unclear • Difficult for audience to name and discern main characters	• Audience understands main character's problem but doesn't understand the significance of the problem • Solution was a little difficult to understand • Audience knows setting, but characteristics of setting are not detailed • Main characters named, but audience knows little about them	• It is fairly easy to understand main character's problem and why it is a problem • Solution is easy to understand and somewhat logical • Vivid words used to express when and where story takes place • Main characters named and described; audience understands them	• Audience clearly understands main character's problem and why it is a problem • Solution is easy to understand and is logical; no loose ends • Many vivid, descriptive words are used to tell the audience when and where the story takes place and what it is like to live there • Audience can describe characters' looks and how they typically behave	___ x 5 = ___ (20) ___ x 5 = ___ (20) ___ x 5 = ___ (20) ___ x 5 = ___ (20)
GRAMMAR • Spelling • Verb conjugations • Complete sentences • Capitalization and punctuation	• 6 or more errors • 6 or more verbs do not match pronouns • 6 or more errors • 6 or more errors	• 4–5 errors • 4–5 verbs do not match pronouns • 4–5 errors • 4–5 errors	• 1–3 errors • 1–3 verbs do not match pronouns • 1–3 errors • 1–3 errors	• Error free • Error free • Error free • Error free	___ x 5 = ___ (20) ___ x 5 = ___ (20) ___ x 5 = ___ (20) ___ x 5 = ___ (20)

COMMENTS:

195–220 = A	
175–194 = B	Final Score ___/(220)
155–174 = C	
130–154 = D	Final Grade ___
0–129 = F	

Thank you to Jennifer Hasler (Westfield High School, Indiana) for providing the ideas for this rubric. (*Standards adapted from Indiana Department of Education. [n.d.]. *Indiana academic standards.* Retrieved March 11, 2004, from http://www.indianastandards.org/)

APPENDIX B

Sample Rubrics

Appendix B includes additional rubrics that follow various different formats that teachers from the Teacher Leadership Academy have developed. Many thanks to the teachers for sharing the assessments they have created. (The Teacher Leadership Academy is sponsored by the Central Indiana Educational Service Center, 6321 LaPas Trail, Indianapolis, Indiana, 46268, 317-387-7100, http://www.ciesc.k12.in.us/.) All rubric artifacts are scans of original teacher-created rubrics that have not been altered.

Teacher Artifact

Fantasy and Reality Unit Rubric
Elementary School Level

Unit Rubric: Fantasy and Reality

Name_____

Created By: Sherry Sigo and Cindy Gregg

Criteria	1 Little Evidence	2 Some Evidence	3 Much Evidence
Demonstrates understanding of reality and fantasy	• No Understanding Demonstrated	• Some Understanding Demonstrated	• Much Understanding Demonstrated
Delivery (oral)	• No Eye Contact • No Gestures • Poorly Organized • Does Not Address Subject	• Some Eye Contact • Some Gestures • Good Organization • Adequately Addresses Subject	• Frequent Eye Contact • Appropriate Gestures • Very Well Organized • Subject Presented Clearly
Delivery (written)	• Incomplete Sentences • Many Punctuation/Capitalization Errors • Many spelling errors • Messy • Poorly Organized • Does Not Address Subject	• Most Sentences Complete • Some Punctuation/Capitalization Errors • Few Spelling Errors • Legible • Good Organization • Adequately Addresses Subject	• Complete Sentence • Correct Punctuation/Capitalization • No Spelling Errors • Neat • Very Well- Organized • Subject Presented Clearly

Grading Scale: 6 points = A   4-5 points = B   3 points =C   2 points = D

Final Score_____

Comments:_____
_____
_____

Thank you to Sherry Sigo and Cindy Gregg (both from Harney Elementary, Lebanon Community Schools, Indiana) for providing this rubric.

Teacher Artifact

Solar System and Stars Project Rubric
Elementary School Level

The Solar System and the Stars Project Rubric

	1	2	3	4
Applies research skills and evaluates information for relevance.	Product shows little or no evidence of research skills, paraphrasing is inadequate.	Product shows inconsistently applied research skills, paraphrasing is mostly effective.	Product shows research skills were generally applied, paraphrasing is well done.	Product shows thoughtfully applied research skills, paraphrasing is exceptional.
Project shows understanding of content.	Limited degree of content understanding shown, may have many mistakes. Irrelevant information is focus of project.	Proficient degree of content understanding fulfills grade-level standard. Extraneous information is sometimes included. Some points not well explained.	Excellent degree of content understanding, good use of supporting details. All information is on topic.	Excellent understanding demonstrated beyond the grasp of main ideas and significant supporting details.
Project is complete, comprehensive, and correct.	Product has many mistakes in spelling, facts, grammar, incomplete information.	Product has several language mistakes, some incorrect information, and is complete.	Product has few mistakes, is complete, and fairly comprehensive.	Product is correct, complete and comprehensive.
Uses graphics effectively	Inadequate use of graphics: may be neat but is not inked or colored, pencil lines may show.	Proficient use of graphics: pleasing to look at, neat, clear, presentable, inked, colored, erased.	Excellent use of graphics: high-quality grade-level work, items placed well in relation to each other.	Exceptional use of graphics: color, shape, lines are neatly and accurately placed, inked, colors , no errors in captions.
Personal Best	Work shows little effort.	Work shows a minimum of effort.	Work shows effort.	Work shows very good effort.

Scoti Bolding and Georgene Koenig
Oaklandon Elementary, MSDLT
TLA 6

Thank you to Scoti Bolding and Georgene Koenig (both from Oaklandon Elementary School, Indiana) for providing this rubric.

Teacher Artifact

Dinosaur Project Rubric
Elementary School Level

Amanda Dillon TLA #6 Unit: Dinosaurs Grade One Rubric	1 Try Again A-Saurus	2 On Your Way A-Saurus	3 Almost A-Saurus	4 DINO-MITE
PRESENTATION	I whispered and did not look at the audience.	I was hard to hear at times and did not have good eye contact.	I spoke loudly enough, but was hard to understand. I had good eye contact most of the time.	I spoke loudly enough and was easy to understand. I had good eye contact all the time.
VISUAL APPEAL	I did not use a visual aid.	My visual aid was sloppy and hard to understand.	My visual aid was neat and logical.	My visual aid was neat, logical, and used effectively.
CONTENT	I did not choose a dinosaur.	I chose a dinosaur, but had inaccurate information.	I chose a dinosaur and used correct and accurate information.	I chose a dinosaur, used correct and accurate information and added details of the habitat and period.
PERSONAL BEST	I did not try. I did not complete the assignment.	I did try, but I did not follow directions. I did not complete the assignment.	I did my best with a complete assignment, but it was messy.	I followed directions and did my best. My assignment was complete and neat.

Thank you to Amanda Dillon (Prairie Trace Elementary, Carmel City Schools, Indiana) for providing this rubric.

Teacher Artifact

Consumerism Role-Play Rubric

Elementary School Level

Submitted by: Christi Linton
Scoring Rubric for Consumerism Unit – Grade 2
Role-Play Activity

Name: _____   Date: _____

Scoring	Criteria
	Voice
	* You were aware of the audience. (You did not turn your back on audience when speaking.)
	* You used a clear voice.
	* You spoke at a good rate, not too fast or too slow.
	* You spoke loudly enough for everyone to hear.
	Presentation and Delivery
	* The moral of the folktale was clearly identified through role-play.
	* The audience was engaged in the role-play.
	* The role-play was clear and focused. (Unimportant information was excluded.)
	* The ideas made sense and flowed with the story.
	* You looked at audience throughout performance.
	Visual Aids
	* You used appropriate props to enhance the role-play.
	* Your visual aids did not interfere with your voice projection.

Scoring Guide:

* **Excellent**
+ **Meets Expectations**
√ **Developing**
• **Additional Learning Experiences Required**

Thank you to Christi Linton (Central Elementary, MSD of Pike Township, Indiana) for providing this rubric.

Teacher Artifact

Chemistry Brochure Rubric
Elementary School Level (Grade 5)

Mary Margaret Gavaghan
Chemistry - Grade 5

Concept Comprehension: Understands chemical change. ____ Gives examples of chemical changes occurring in our world. ____ States effects of chemical changes.	5. Exceptional presentation of brochure near professional quality. 4. Excellent presentation of brochure exceeds grade level work. 3. Proficient presentation gives clear evidence of concepts. 2. Inadequate presentation of brochure weak or unclear evidence of concepts. 1. Incomplete presentation of conceptual knowledge.
Drawing Conclusions: Draws appropriate conclusions from information. ____ Explains human impact of chemical change. ____ Give examples of remedies or benefits for chemicals.	5. Exceptional ideas of chemical use. Original thinking. 4. Excellent ideas of chemical use. Common but complete. 3. Proficient ideas. Common thinking. 2. Inadequate ideas of chemical use. Incorrect or impossible conclusions. 1. Incomplete ideas. Few or not ideas stated.
Visual Communication: Attractive visual presentation. ____ Visuals use the space and paper well. ____ Visuals are neat and presentable. ____ Text is appropriate for visuals. ____ Spelling and grammar is correct.	5. Exceptional art and language use. Near professional quality. 4. Excellent art and language use. Above grade level quality. 3. Proficient use of art and language. Grade level quality. 2. Inadequate use of art and language work lacks neatness and or contains language errors. 1. Incomplete use of art or language. Brochure uses no art or contains frequent language errors.

Thank you to Mary Margaret Gavaghan (Amy Beverland Elementary, MSD of Lawrence Township, Indiana) for providing this rubric.

Teacher Artifact

Middle Ages Rubric
Middle School Level

Middle Ages Rubric

Cyndi Brown   TLA6   Speedway Schools

Important People

Identifies contributions	▪ 5 – Exceptional understanding of societal roles and their impacts. Work is beyond grade level.
Connects to an event	▪ 4 – Excellent understanding of roles. Higher grade level work.
Identifies impact on society	▪ 3 – Proficient understanding of roles with key information missing or incomplete. Grade level work.
Chooses relevant information	
Information is accurate	▪ 2 – Inadequate understanding of roles. Key pieces are missing or incorrect. Lower grade level.
	▪ 1 – Poor effort or understanding. Below grade level.

Important Events

Chooses relevant information	▪ 5 – Exceptional understanding of importance of events. Work is beyond grade level.
Connects to other events	▪ 4 – Excellent understanding of importance of events. Higher grade level work.
Identifies causes and effects	▪ 3 – Proficient understanding of events with key pieces missing or incomplete. Work is grade level.
Information is accurate	▪ 2 – Inadequate understanding of events with information missing or incorrect. Lower grade level.
Critical details are included	
	▪ 1 – Poor effort or understanding. Work is below grade level.

Inventions / Legacies

Information is accurate	▪ 5 – Exceptional understanding of inventions / discoveries and their impact on medieval society and society of today:. Work is beyond grade level.
Information is relevant	▪ 4 – Excellent understanding of inventions / discoveries and their impact. Higher grade level work.
Impact on society is identified	▪ 3 – Proficient understanding of inventions / legacies and their impacts: key pieces missing or incomplete. Grade level work.
Impact on modern society is identified	▪ 2 – Inadequate understanding of inventions of the Medieval period with inadequate or incomplete information. Lower grade level work.
Description is included	
	▪ 1 – Poor effort or understanding. Work is below grade level.

Presentation

Neat	▪ 5 – Presentation conveys exceptional understanding / interpretation of material. Presentation is professional quality. No errors. Work is beyond grade level.
Correct language mechanics	▪ 4 – Presentation conveys excellent understanding of information. Presentation is high quality. No errors. High grade level work.
Appealing visual presentation	▪ 3 – Proficient understanding is demonstrated by the presentation. Few errors. Grade level work.
Graphics used effectively	▪ 2 – Inadequate understanding of the material is demonstrated. Presentation is sloppy. Errors are present. Lower grade level work.
Components are captioned or labeled	
	▪ 1 – Presentation demonstrates poor effort or understanding. Sloppy with many errors. Work is below grade level.

Thank you to Cyndi Brown (Wheeler Elementary, Speedway City Schools, Indiana) for providing this rubric.

Teacher Artifact

Restless Earth: Pragmatic Performance Rubric
Middle School Level (Grade 8)

Sheila Cobb
The Restless Earth
Grade 8

ACTIVITY: Students will write an editorial essay to the newspapers of an ancient society, persuading them to view volcanoes from a new scientific point of view.

TRAIT 1 Understands and interprets historical events

___ States key historical events	**4 EXCEPTIONAL degree of understanding:** ➢ Exceptional interpretation of event ➢ Analysis surpasses grade-level expectations
	3 EXCELLENT degree of understanding: ➢ Excellent interpretation of event ➢ Analysis represents high-quality grade-level work
___ Identifies fact vs. fiction	**2 AVERAGE degree of understanding:** ➢ Average interpretation of event ➢ Analysis fulfills grade-level standard
___ Includes critical details	**1 LIMITED degree of understanding:** ➢ Minimal interpretation of event ➢ Bare-bones analysis makes it below grade level
___ Specifies setting (time and place)	**0 MISSING degree of understanding:** ➢ No attempt to complete task as assigned

Thank you to Sheila Cobb (Belzer Middle School, MSD of Lawrence Township, Indiana) for providing this rubric.

Teacher Artifact

Astronomy Unit: NASA Video Rubric
Middle School Level

Sue Engledow
Astronomy Unit
Divergent Thinking

Create and direct a video highlighting the accomplishments of NASA and its future goals.

Trait 1   Demonstrates a knowledge of the history/plans of NASA

____ **Presents important information about dates & highlights of NASA history** ____ **Information is accurate** ____ **Information is thorough enough to indicate an understanding of NASA's program**	**5** Excellent understanding/interpretation of events: analysis represents high-quality grade-level work **4** Proficient understanding/interpretation of events: analysis fulfills grade-level standards **3** Inadequate degree of understanding of these events: attempted analysis, but missing key pieces **2** Limited degree of understanding of these events: bare-bones analysis makes it below grade level **1** Missing degree of understanding of this event: no attempt to complete task as assigned	

Trait 2   Communicates ideas effectively through video format

____ **Information is presented in a logical order** ____ **Video holds the viewers' interest** ____ **Audio & video fit together**	**5** Excellent degree of use of video techniques; high quality grade-level work; professional, high-quality video **4** Proficient degree of use of video techniques; fulfills grade-level standards **3** Inadequate degree of use of video techniques; falls short of grade-level standards **2** Limited degree of use of video techniques; falls below grade-level standards **1** Missing degree of understanding of use of video techniques; completely misses the mark	

Trait 3   Video demonstrates creativity

____ **Information is presented in an interesting manner** ____ **Visual presentation supplements the information presented**	**5** Excellent degree of creativity displayed; high quality grade-level standards **4** Proficient degree of creativity displayed; fulfills grade-level standards **3** Inadequate degree of creativity displayed; falls short of grade-level standards **2** Limited degree of creativity displayed; falls below grade-level standards **1** Missing degree of creativity; no creativity displayed	

Thank you to Sue Engledow (Clay Jr. High School, Carmel City Schools, Indiana) for providing this rubric.

Teacher Artifact

Civil War Persuasive Writing Rubric
Middle School Level (Grade 8)

Lynn Cox
Civil War Unit – Grade 8

Trait 1   Understands and interprets historical events   _____

_____ States key historical information
_____ Identifies regional prejudice
_____ Includes critical details
_____ Information is accurate

5. *excellent* degree of content understanding represents high-quality grade-level work:
   • Thorough and accurate grasp of main ideas and significant supporting details
4. *proficient* degree of content understanding fulfills grade-level standard:
   • Indicates an understanding of main ideas and relevant specific supporting details
3. *inadequate* degree of content understanding falls a bit short:
   • Correctly identifies some main ideas, focuses on isolated details or omits some significant details
2. *limited* degree of content understanding falls below grade level:
   • Shows a fragmented, inaccurate or incomplete understanding, presents random, incomplete, or irrelevant evidence
1. *missing* degree of content understanding completely misses the mark:
   • No attempt to complete task as assigned

Trait 2   Developing a convincing argument   _____

_____ States point of view clearly
_____ Offers full reasoning to support position
_____ Uses a strong organizational strategy
_____ Uses elaborative details

5. *excellent* development of your point of view:
   • Persuasion goes well beyond grade-level expectations
4. *proficient* development of your point of view:
   • Persuasion fulfills grade-level standard
3. *inadequate* development of your point of view:
   • Attempted persuasion, but missing key pieces
2. *limited* development of your point of view:
   • Failed persuasion makes it below grade level
1. *missing* development of your point of view:
   • No attempt at persuasion

Trait 3   Controls conventions of writing   _____

_____ Correct grammar & usage contribute to clarity
_____ Sound paragraphing reinforces organization
_____ Correct spelling
_____ Correct capitalization and punctuation

5. *excellent* control of writing conventions
   • Mechanics go way beyond grade-level expectations
4. *proficient* control of writing conventions:
   • Some errors, but mechanics fulfill grade-level standard
3. *inadequate* control of writing conventions:
   • Attempted mechanics, but errors interrupt reading
2. *limited* control of writing conventions:
   • Too many mechanical errors cause confusion for reader
1. *missing* control of writing conventions:
   • No attempt to repair mechanical errors as assigned

Thank you to Lynn Cox (Clay Jr. High School, Carmel City Schools, Indiana) for providing this rubric.

Teacher Artifact

Algebra Help Web Sites Rubric
Middle School Level (Algebra 1)

Algebra 1 Project 5th Six Weeks
Using Algebra Help Websites – Score Sheet

Name _____

Block _____

Content (Mathematical)	All	Most	Some	None
Correctly makes 3 original polynomial multiplication problems				
Correctly determines whether given polynomials factor by the trinomial, difference of squares, or GCF method				
Gives correct examples of binomials				
Correctly answers questions about FOIL using algebra help websites				
Correctly answers practice problems				

Content (Computer)	All	Most	Some	None
Follows directions to arrive at proper website and proper page				
Correctly prints practice problems from website				
Correctly uses FOIL "calculator"				
Knows keystrokes for inputting quadratics				
Correctly uses Polynomial Multiplication "calculator"				
Correctly uses Factoring "solver"				
Correctly uses Power of Polynomials "solver"				
Correctly documents websites with title, author, URL and date				
Conducts and prints a successful MSN search using 'algebra help' as key words				
Column Totals				

ALL =4, MOST = 3, SOME = 2, NONE = 1

TOTAL POINTS _____

Thank you to Janeen Godfrey for providing this rubric.

Teacher Artifact

DNA and Protein Synthesis Board Game Rubric
High School Level

Marva Moore
TLA-6

DNA/Protein Synthesis Unit
Board Game Rubric

Criteria	1	2	3	4
Historical Reserch/ Scientists	*Very little information on research history and scientists	*A few questions on history & scientists included	*Several questions on history & scientists included	*All scientists mentioned in the unit & major research included
DNA/RNA Structure	*Components of DNA/ RNA	*Components & structure of DNA/RNA	*Components, structure, & comparisons of DNA/RNA	*Components, structure, comparisons, & bonding of DNA/RNA
DNA Replication	*Defined	*Defined, outcome covered	*Defined, steps covered	*Defined, steps covered connection to mutations made
Protein Synthesis	*Defined	*Defined, transcription, & translation mentioned	*Defined, transcription, & translation steps covered	*Defined, transcription, & translation steps covered, connection to mutations made
DNA & Mendel's Principles Connection	*Mendel mentioned	*Mendel mentined, DNA/gene connection made	Mendel mentioned, DNA/gene connection & gene-protein synthesis connection made	Mendel mentioned connection between DNA-gene-protein synthesis-phenotype made
Board Game Aesthetics	*Messy, not well thought out, parts missing	*Functional, all parts included	*Neatly done, colorful, all parts included	*Creative, colorful, all parts included, engaging
Board Game Usability	*Would not clarify content very thoroughly	*Covers most topics	*Provides good review of information	*Leads students to making connections

Thank you to Marva Moore (Hamilton Southeastern High School, Hamilton Southeastern Schools, Indiana) for providing this rubric.

Teacher Artifact

Genetics Rubric
High School Level

Scoring/Criteria	1	2	3	4	Score
Terminology * Number of vocabulary words used	Less than 3 words	3-5 words	6-8 words	9-10 words	__ x 6 = __ (24)
Use of Punnett Square * Show sample cross	Copied and incorrect	Original cross; wrong pattern	Copied; correct inheritance pattern	Original; correct inheritance pattern	__ x 4 = __ (16)
Use of pedigree * Show inheritance pattern * Use symbols and structures correctly	* Copied and incorrect * More than 2 errors	* Original cross; wrong pattern * 2 errors	* Copied; correct inheritance pattern * 1 error	* Original; correct inheritance pattern * 0 errors	[row 3] __ x 2 = __ (8) __ x 2 = __ (8)
Probability * Use of percent or fraction to impart chance of inheritance	Inaccurate	Accurate, but does not explain its origin nor the relationship to future generations	Accurate, but does not explain either the origin of the number or its relationship to future generations	Accurate and explains how the percent came to be and its relationship to future generations	__ x 1 = __ (4)
Biotechnology * Explanation of technology * Indication of use in specific and topic-related situation	* Only mentioned * Only mentioned	* Missing procedure or application * Example is missing detail and relevance	* Technology procedure and application explained, but lacking detail * Example lacks relevant detail	* Technology procedure and application explained in detail * Specific real-world example included	__ x 1 = __ (4) __ x 1 = __ (4)
Presentation * Address of subject * Speech volume, eye contact, and body language * Organization	* Poor * Poor * Poor	* Fair * Fair * Fair	* Good * Good * Good	* Super * Super * Super	__ x 1 = __ (4) __ x 1 = __ (4) __ x 1 = __ (4)
Structure * Originality * Visuals	* Poor * Poor	* Fair * Fair	* Good * Good	* Super * Super	__ x 1 = __ (4) __ x 1 = __ (4)

Final Score: ____/(92)

Thank you to Andrea Stonemaker (Lawrence Central High School, MSD of Lawrence Township, Indiana) for providing this rubric.

Teacher Artifact

Travel Brochure Rubric
High School Level

Scoring Rubric for Travel Brochure

Name:_____ Date:_____

Teacher	Student	Prewriting Skills
		Viewed and compared various brochures thoroughly
		Located and gathered information from the internet
		Located information from travel agencies or state's chamber of commerce
		Located information from library books, encyclopedias, magazines, etc.
		Organized information into at least 7 categories, such as location, map, sports...
		Collected and/or drew pictures/photos to add to your brochure
		Set up Word Brochure format or selected paper to use for brochure

Teacher	Student	Organization of information
		Includes at least 7 categories
		Includes pictures that add clarity, interest and information
		Includes a title
		Includes subtitles/categories
		Categories placed in an organized manner

Teacher	Student	Responding and Revising
		Received and utilized feedback from at least one other person
		Offered beneficial feedback to at least one of your peers
		Final brochure shows significant improvement compared to original draft
		Checked and followed project guidelines

Teacher	Student	Writing conventions
		Correct spelling is used
		Correct capitalization is used
		Correct punctuation is used
		Appropriate grammar is used
		Uses complete sentences which contain subject and verb agreement

Teacher	Student	Overall appearance
		Various fonts and sizes of fonts used
		Colorful and appealing pictures and print
		Easy to read and understand
		Original and creative

Mastery	Non-Mastery (additional learning experiences needed)
6 Wow! Exceptional! Professional Looking! Pah!	3 Marginal, So-So, Progressing
5 Great! Excellent!	2 Poor work, Limited
4 Good! Proficient!	1 Incomplete, Missing

Submitted by Toni A. Wolfe 4-26-01

Thank you to Toni A. Wolfe for providing this rubric.

Teacher Artifact

Back to the Future: Historical Fiction and Current Research Rubric
High School Level

Back to the Future—Historical Fiction and Current Research Rubric

Name: _____ Period: ____

Summarize Historical Fiction- one paragraph	5. Excellent
_____ Selects appropriate historical fiction	4. Meets expectations
_____ Follows BGMS process writing format	3. Needs improvement
_____ Spelling and grammar are correct	2. Partial completion
	1. Incomplete
Compose Questions	5. Excellent
_____ Identifies correct historical period	4. Meets expectations
_____ Determines 5 historical questions	3. Needs improvement
_____ Questions are thoughtful	2. Partial completion
_____ Questions relate to more several subject areas	1. Incomplete
Complete Booknotes	5. Excellent descriptions
_____ Describes Characters	4. Descriptions meet expectations
_____ Describes Plot and Conflicts	3. Lacks details
_____ Describes Theme	2. Partial completion
	1. Incomplete
Literary Response and Analysis	5. Excellent
_____ Follows BGMS writing format	4. Meets expectations
_____ Accurate grammar and spelling	3. Lacks details
_____ Student provides support for his/her opinions using facts from the text	2. Partial completion
_____ Student distinguishes between fact and fiction	1. Incomplete
Locate and Restate historical facts to support the historical fiction	5. Excellent
_____ Print sources are used	4. Meets expectations
_____ Online sources are used	3. Lacks details
_____ Questions are answered/or facts are given related to the historical period	2. Partial completion
	1. Incomplete
Design Visual	5. Excellent planning
_____ Storyboard complete containing summary of historical fiction, questions, literary response, and historical facts related to their historical fiction	4. Good planning
	3. Planning lacks details
_____ Storyboard is neat and readable	2. Partial completion
	1. Incomplete
Class Presentation	5. Excellent
_____ Student displays enthusiasm	4. Meets expectations
_____ Student demonstrates appropriate voice, gestures and poise	3. Needs improvement
_____ Student understands relations of fact and fiction	2. Partial completion
_____ Appropriate use of visuals	1. Incomplete
Cite Sources Used	5. Accurately follows format, accurate punctuation, and list in alphabetical order
_____ Follows BGMS Bibliographic format for print sources	4. Format followed
_____ Follows BGMS Bibliographic format for online sources	3. Format followed, with several errors
	2. Partial list
	1. Incomplete
_____ **Total Points (125 points possible)**	

Thank you to Barbara Hult (Beech Grove Middle School, Beech Grove City Schools, Indiana) for providing this rubric.

Bibliography

Andrade, H. G. (2000). Using rubrics to promote thinking and learning. *Educational Leadership, 57*(5), 13–18.

Assessment that informs practice [Issue title; Electronic version]. (2000). *ENC Focus, 7*(2). Retrieved February 26, 2004, from http://enc.org/focus/ assessment

Banks, J. C. (1997). *Creating and assessing performance-based curriculum projects: A teacher's guide to project-based learning and performance assessment.* Edmonds, WA: CATS Publications.

Barr, R. D., & Parrett, W. (2003). *Saving our students, saving our schools.* Glenview, IL: Pearson Professional Development.

Black, P., & William, D. (1998). Inside the black box: Raising standards through classroom assessment. *Phi Delta Kappan, 79*(8), 139–148.

Bransford, J., Brown, A. L., & Cocking, R. R. (Eds.). (2000). *How people learn: Brain, mind, experience, and school.* Washington, DC: National Academy Press.

Burke, K. (1999). *The mindful school: How to assess authentic learning.* Arlington Heights, IL: SkyLight Training and Publishing.

Burke, K. (Ed.). (2002). *Mentoring guidebook level 2: Exploring teaching strategies.* Thousand Oaks, CA: Corwin Press.

Caine, R. N., & Caine, G. (1994). *Making connections: Teaching and the human brain.* New York: Addison-Wesley.

Carr, J. F., & Harris, D. E. (2001). *Succeeding with standards: Linking curriculum, assessments, and action planning.* Alexandria, VA: Association for Supervision and Curriculum Development.

Carter, R., & Frith, C. D. (2000). *Mapping the mind.* Berkeley: University of California Press.

Collins, J. (2001). *Good to great.* New York: HarperCollins.

Cotton, K. (2000). *The schooling practices that matter most.* Portland, OR: Northwest Regional Education Laboratory.

Darling-Hammond, L. (1997). *The right to learn: A blueprint for creating schools that work.* San Francisco: Jossey-Bass.

Depka, E. (2001). *Designing rubrics for mathematics.* Thousand Oaks, CA: Corwin Press.

Diamond, M. (1988). *Enriching heredity: The impact of the environment on the brain.* New York: Free Press.

Donovan, M. S., Bransford, J. D., & Pellegrino, J. W. (Eds.). (1999). *How people learn: Bridging research and practice.* Washington, DC: Committee on Learning Research and Educational Practice, National Research Council.

Easton, L. B. (2002). *The other side of curriculum.* Portsmouth, NH: Heinemann.

Farr, B. P., & Trumbell, E. (1997). *Assessment alternatives for diverse classrooms.* Norwood, MA: Christopher-Gordon.

Fogarty, R. (1991). *The mindful school: How to integrate the curricula.* Palatine, IL: IRI/Skylight Publishing.

Fogarty, R. (1997). *Problem-based learning and other curriculum models for the multiple intelligences classroom.* Thousand Oaks, CA: Corwin Press.

Foriska, T. J. (1998). *Restructuring around standards: A practitioner's guide to design and implementation.* Thousand Oaks, CA: Corwin.

Gardner, H. (1983). *Frames of mind: The theory of multiple intelligences.* New York: Basic.

Gardner, H. (1993). *Multiple intelligences: The theory in practice.* New York: Basic.

Goleman, D. (1995). *Emotional intelligence: Why it can matter more than IQ.* New York: Bantam.

Good, T. L., & Brophy, J. E. (1997). *Looking in classrooms* (7th ed.). New York: Longman.

Guskey, T. R. (1997). *Implementing mastery learning* (2nd ed.). Belmont, CA: Wadsworth Press.

Hill, B. C., Ruptic, C., & Norwick, L. (1998). *Classroom based assessment.* Norwood, MA: Christopher-Gordon.

Hunter, M. (1981). *Teaching for transfer.* El Segundo, CA: TIP Publication.

Hunter, M. (1995). *Mastery teaching: Increasing instructional effectiveness in elementary and secondary schools, colleges, and universities.* Thousand Oaks, CA: Corwin.

Illinois State Board of Education. (1995). *Effective scoring rubrics: A guide to their use and development.* Springfield, IL: Author.

Indiana Department of Education. (n.d.). *Indiana academic standards.* Retrieved March 8, 2004, from http://www.indianastandards.org/

Jacobs, H. H. (1997). *Mapping the big picture.* Alexandria, VA: Association for Supervision and Curriculum Development.

Jacobs, H. H. (Ed.). (1989). *Interdisciplinary curriculum: Design and implementation.* Alexandria, VA: Association for Supervision and Curriculum Development.

Johnson, D. W., Johnson, R. T., & Holubec, E. J. (1986). *Circles of learning: Cooperation in the classroom.* Edina, MN: Interaction.

Joyce, B., Weil, M., & Calhoun, E. (2004). *Models of teaching* (7th ed.). Boston: Allyn and Bacon.

LeDoux, J. (1998). *The emotional brain: The mysterious underpinning of emotional life.* New York: Simon and Schuster.

Levine, M. D. (2002). *A mind at a time.* New York: Simon and Schuster.

Lewin, L., & Shoemaker, B. J. (1998). *Great performances: Creating classroom-based assessment tasks.* Alexandria, VA: Association for Supervision and Curriculum Development.

Lockery, T. (n.d.). Starting at the right end: Planning backwards [Electronic version]. *The Seattle Press.* Retrieved February 26, 2004, from http://www.seattlepress.com/article-9495.html

Marzano, R. J. (1999). Building curriculum and assessment around standards. *The High School Magazine, 6*(5), 14–19.

Marzano, R. J. (2000). *Transforming classroom grading.* Alexandria, VA: Association for Supervision and Curriculum Development.

Marzano, R. J., & Kendall, J. S. (1996). *A comprehensive guide to designing standards-based districts, schools, and classrooms.* Aurora, CO: Mid-continent Regional Educational Laboratory.

Marzano, R. J., & Pickering, D. (1997). *Dimensions of learning: Trainer's manual* (2nd ed.). Alexandria, VA: Association for Supervision and Curriculum Development; Aurora, CO: Mid-continent Regional Educational Laboratory.

Marzano, R. J., Pickering, D. J., & Pollock, J. E. (2001). *Classroom instruction that works: Research-based strategies for increasing student achievement.* Alexandria, VA: Association for Supervision and Curriculum Development.

National Board for Professional Teaching Standards. (n.d.). *What teachers should know and be able to do: The five core propositions of the National Board.* Retrieved February 26, 2004, from http://www.nbpts.org/about/coreprops.cfm

National Partnership for Excellence and Accountability in Teaching. (n.d.). *Projects and activities.* Retrieved February 26, 2004, from http://ed-web3.educ.msu.edu/npeat/projects.htm

National Research Council. (2000). *How people learn: Brain, mind, experience, and school.* Washington, DC: National Academy Press.

Nelson, K., & Lindley, K. (2004). *Starting strong: Surviving and thriving as a new teacher.* Glenview, IL: Pearson Professional Development.

Newmann, F. M., Secada, W. G., & Wehlage, G. G. (1995). *Guide to authentic instruction and assessment: Vision, standards, and scoring.* Madison: Wisconsin Center for Educational Research, University of Wisconsin.

Nitko, A. J. (2001). *Educational assessment of students* (3rd ed.). Upper Saddle River, NJ: Prentice Hall.

Ogle, D. (1986). K-W-L: A teaching model that develops active reading of expository text. *The Reading Teacher, 37*(6), 564–570.

Parry, T., & Gregory, G. (1998). *Designing brain-compatible learning.* Thousand Oaks, CA: Corwin Press.

Pomperaug Regional School District 15. (1996). *A teacher's guide to performance-based learning and assessment.* Alexandria, VA: Association for Supervision and Curriculum Development.

Popham, W. J. (1999). *Classroom assessment: What teachers need to know.* Needham Heights, MA: Allyn and Bacon.

Prince George's County Public Schools, Region II Administrative Office. (2003, September 9). *Rubric basics.* Retrieved February 26, 2004, from http://www.pgcps.pg.k12.md.us/~region2/assessment_rubrics.htm

Renzulli, J. S. (2001). *Enriching curriculum for all students.* Thousand Oaks, CA: Corwin Press.

Ripoll, T. (1999). Why this made me think of that. *Thinking and Reasoning, 4*(10), 15–43.

Ronis, D. (2001). *Problem-based learning for math and science.* Thousand Oaks, CA: Corwin Press.

Ronis, D. (2002). *Clustering standards in integrated units.* Thousand Oaks, CA: Corwin Press.

Schmoker, M. (1996). *Results.* Alexandria, VA: Association for Supervision and Curriculum Development.

Schmoker, M. (2001). *The results handbook.* Alexandria, VA: Association for Supervision and Curriculum Development.

Senge, P. M. (2000). *A fifth discipline: Schools that learn.* New York: Doubleday.

Silver, H. F., Strong, R. W., & Perini, M. J. (2000). *So each may learn: Integrating learning styles and multiple intelligences.* Alexandria, VA: Association for Supervision and Curriculum Development.

Smith, J. K., Smith, L. F., & De Lisi, R. (2001). *Natural classroom assessment: Designing seamless instruction and assessment.* Thousand Oaks, CA: Corwin.

Sprenger, M. B. (2002). *Becoming a "wiz" at brain-based teaching: From translation to application. How to make every year your best year.* Thousand Oaks, CA: Corwin.

Stiggins, R. J. (1994). *Student-centered classroom assessment.* New York: Merrill.

Stiggins, R. J. (2001). *Student-involved classroom assessment.* Saddle River, NJ: Prentice Hall.

Strong, R. W., Silver, H. F., & Perini, M. J. (2001). *Teaching what matters most: Standards and strategies for raising student achievement.* Alexandria, VA: Association for Supervision and Curriculum Development.

Sylwester, R. (Ed.). (1998). *Student brains, school issues: A collection of articles.* Thousand Oaks, CA: Corwin Press.

Tapscott, D. (1999). Educating the Net generation. *Educational Leadership, 56*(5), 6–11.

Tomlinson, C. A. (1999). *The differentiated classroom: Responding to the needs of all learners.* Alexandria, VA: Association for Supervision and Curriculum Development.

US Department of Education. (1998). *Promising practices: New ways to improve teacher quality.* Washington, DC: Author. Retrieved February 26, 2004, from http://www.ed.gov/pubs/PromPractice/index.html

West, T. (1997). *In the mind's eye: Visual thinkers, gifted people with dyslexia and other learning difficulties, computer images and the ironies of creativity.* Amherst, NY: Prometheus.

Wiggins, G. (1998). *Educative assessment: Designing assessments to inform and improve student performance.* San Francisco: Jossey-Bass.

Wiggins, G., & McTighe, J. (1998). *Understanding by design.* Alexandria, VA: Association for Supervision and Curriculum Development.

Williams, B. R., & Dunn, S. (2000). *Brain-compatible learning for the block.* Thousand Oaks, CA: Corwin Press.

Wolfe, P. (2001). *Brain matters: Translating research into classroom practice.* Alexandria, VA: Association for Supervision and Curriculum Development.

Index

CORWIN PRESS